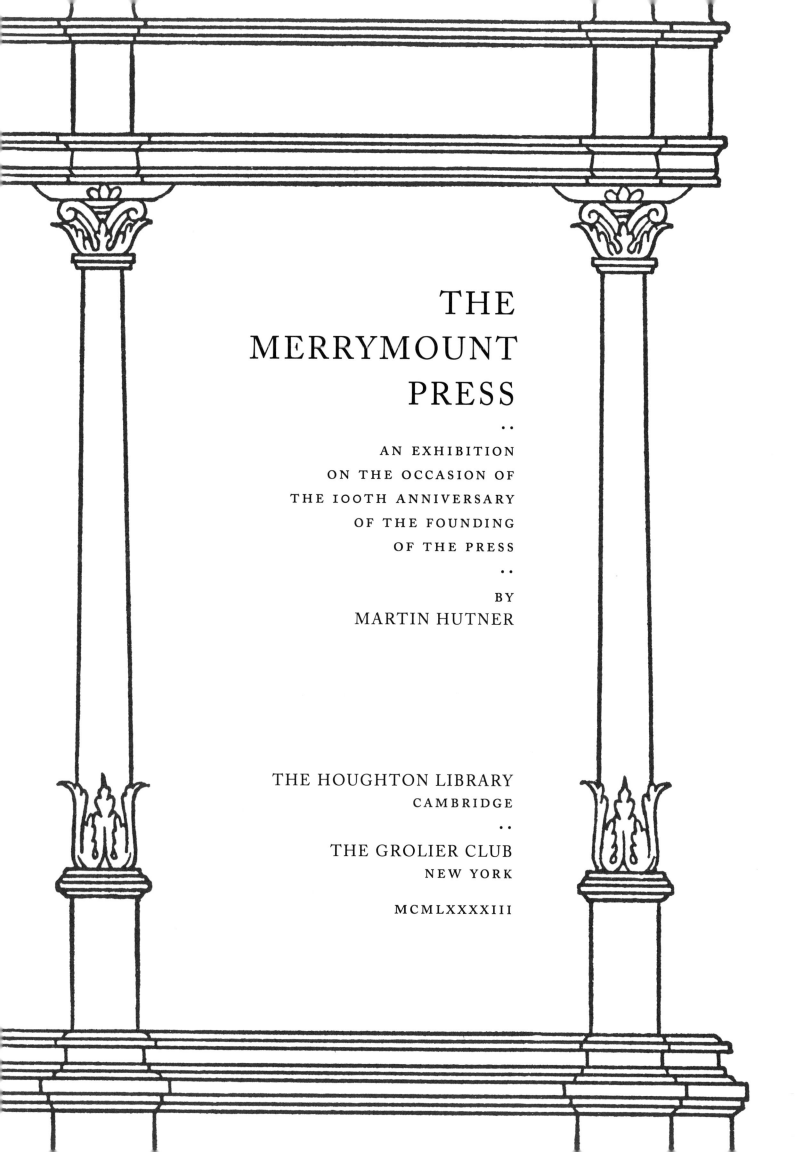

THE MERRYMOUNT PRESS

..

AN EXHIBITION
ON THE OCCASION OF
THE 100TH ANNIVERSARY
OF THE FOUNDING
OF THE PRESS

..

BY
MARTIN HUTNER

THE HOUGHTON LIBRARY
CAMBRIDGE

..

THE GROLIER CLUB
NEW YORK

MCMLXXXXIII

THE BORDER ON THE TITLE-PAGE
HAS BEEN ADAPTED FROM THE PROSPECTUS
PRINTED AT THE MERRYMOUNT PRESS
FOR THE HUMANISTS' LIBRARY, 1906.

FOREWORD

. .

THE YEAR PRECEDING D. B. Updike's death, 1940, was of great significance both to him and to his Merrymount Press. Lectures, exhibitions, and talks succeeded one another on the East as well as the West coast. Perhaps most outstanding among these were the events at Harvard and The Grolier Club.

Updike had become a member of the Grolier Club in 1893, the year he founded the Press. Highly regarded by his New York peers, he was awarded an honorary membership in 1926. Updike printed over the years some of the Club's most attractive publications; and the Club, to honor the octogenarian, held a major retrospective of Updike's work in March of 1940, jointly sponsored with the American Insititue of Graphic Arts.

Just a few weeks before, in a similar spirit of respect and admiration, Philip Hofer, founder of the Department of Printing and Graphic Arts at Harvard, had invited Updike to give two talks to the Friends of the Harvard College Library. Updike's association with Harvard had begun in 1911, with a series of lectures on the technique of printing for the Graduate School of Business Administration. These lectures formed the basis of *Printing Types*, his monumental work on typography published by Harvard University Press in 1922, for which Updike was awarded an honorary master's degree in 1929.

Updike's talks for the Friends of the Harvard College Library, revealingly entitled "The Essentials of a Well-Made Book," and "The Place of the Educated Man in the Printing Industry," were delivered to an overflow audience in the upper Treasure Room of the Widener Library in January of 1940. One may well imagine Philip Hofer's disappointment at having to relinquish their publication, "the war having so intensified our financial problems for the 'Friends' that we feel we cannot appropriate as much money to print these as would be necessary."

It could not be more appropriate, nor we believe could it give Philip Hofer more pleasure if he were still with us today, than for the Houghton Library and for The Grolier Club to join in celebrating the centenary of D. B. Updike's Merrymount Press. On exhibition at the Houghton Library during April and May, and at the Grolier from September through November, 1993, are some one hundred and thirty works spanning the range of his career and of the life of the Press, from 1891 to 1949.

Half a century has elapsed since the Grolier retrospective. What was regarded then as the accomplishment of the Scholar Printer, "his unfailing correctness of taste and style and his perfection of execution," has passed the test of time. More than anything else, today's exhibition demonstrates the enduring relevance of this accomplishment. The quiet genius of Updike, whose program for himself and the Press was "to do the ordinary work of its day well, . . . suitably for the purpose that it is intended, and . . . better than other people think worth while," still shines through. At the end of his own life, Updike already perceived "anxious days when skies seem falling and we are teased by problems that we cannot solve"; for us, who since then have also lived through decades of typographical experimentation, deconstruction, and major technological changes, the forceful presence of Updike's volumes–their striking yet restrained beauty–reaffirms the validity of, and satisfies our longing for, the classical ideals of clarity, order, and harmonious proportion.

Martin Hutner's exhibition reacquaints us in an intimate manner with Updike the man while it also throws new light on the work of the Press. The catalogue for this exhibition, together with his recently published *The Making of the Book of Common Prayer of 1928*, marks the culmination of fifteen years of passionate research on the part of Martin Hutner, research that has made him, indisputably, one of the pre-eminent scholars and bibliographers of D. B. Updike and his Press.

Updike himself, we believe, would have approved of Jerry Kelly's handsome and restrained design for the catalogue; so would he have admired the beautiful way in which it is printed by The Stinehour Press. To each of these collaborators, we are indebted.

Anne Anninger
Philip Hofer Curator of Printing & Graphic Arts
Houghton Library, Harvard University

Martin Antonetti
Librarian, The Grolier Club

ACKNOWLEDGEMENTS

. .

IN MANY WAYS the year 1993 seemed as far away to me at the inception of this project as the year 1893. Inexorably, the years peeled away at an astonishing, accelerating rate, and suddenly I was both curator and writer in a maelstrom of activity. This seems to be the nature of all things planned years in advance. And it also seems in the nature of things that one cannot undertake an enterprise of this dimension without the help, support, and expertise of friends and colleagues.

There is one friend and colleague to whom I owe more than I will ever be able to express adequately, and that person is the late Robert Nikirk, former Librarian of The Grolier Club. Bob encouraged me in everything I did in the world of books. He championed the idea of a Merrymount exhibition, for he personally admired the work of the Press. His enthusiasm, his love of books and of The Grolier Club, his charm, wit, and personal intelligence are all part of my affectionate memory of him, and form part of the impetus for this exhibition. It is, therefore, to Bob's memory with deep appreciation that I dedicate this work.

And it is also with pleasure and appreciation that I thank Bob's successor, Martin Antonetti, who has brought his own particular knowledge and expertise to this project. Our friend and Club President Kenneth Lohf has been encouraging and supportive, ultimately ensuring the publication of this catalogue. Kimball Higgs has made significant and helpful discoveries, and William McClure has lent a useful hand. To these friends and colleagues at The Grolier Club, my thanks and warm appreciation.

At Harvard's Houghton Library, Roger Stoddard's early suggestion of using my collection in New York and the Houghton Merrymount Press Harding collection in Cambridge made the idea of a dual exhibition feasible. His early encouragement and professional precision set the project on a firmer basis. Anne Anninger, with whom I worked in Cambridge, provided what were ideal conditions. Her assiduous and informed preparations, her knowledge, energy, practicality, and skill made my task a total pleasure. For me she is the consummate curator. Over all these activities, Richard Wendorf has extended gracious encouragement. Harvard's generous initial support of this catalogue enabled it to become a permanent record of the exhibition.

I am grateful to Philip Weimerskirch, Curator of Special Collections at the Providence Public Library, for his help and interest, and for permission to quote from unpublished letters; as well as to Ralph Franklin and Patricia Willis of Yale University for assistance, and for permission to quote from an Updike letter. For information and advice, thanks are due Kit Currie, Francis Mattson, Paul Needham, Stephen Stinehour, Alice Beckwith, Henry Beckwith, and Jill Erickson and John Lannon of the Boston Athenaeum. I am also indebted to the Monadnock Paper Company and to Murray E.

Grant, Manager, advertising sales promotion, The Strathmore Paper Company for their contribution towards this publication; and to Kathryn Talalay, who has edited the catalogue with patience and skill.

Finally, to my good friend Jerry Kelly (whose appreciation of Updike has been one of our happiest bonds) for his encouragement, suggestions, information, and enthusiasm—to say nothing of the expected but nonetheless brilliance of his design for this catalogue—I say thank-you in 100-point type.

M.H.

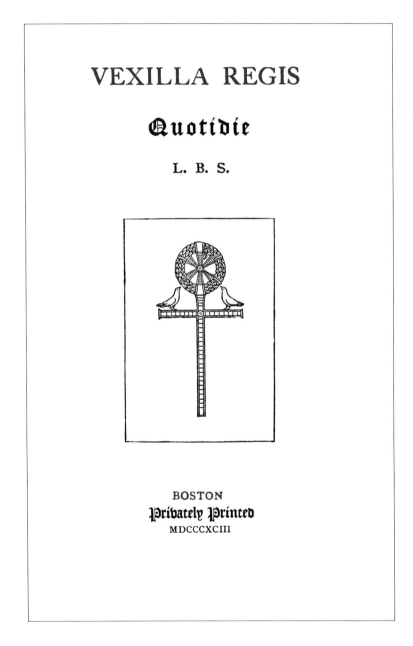

THE FIRST BOOK OF THE MERRYMOUNT PRESS

INTRODUCTION

· ·

DANIEL BERKELEY UPDIKE, who founded The Merrymount Press of Boston in 1893, was born in 1860 in Providence, Rhode Island. He was the son of Caesar Augustus Updike, one-time presiding officer of the Rhode Island House of Representatives, and of Elizabeth Bigelow Adams, of Worcester, Massachusetts. Daniel was descended from both Dutch and English colonists. His ancestors were among the earliest settlers of Rhode Island, and their descendants were to become some of the most prominent families in New England.

The death of Daniel's father in 1877 left his family in severe financial difficulties, and the young man, denied the possibility of a college education, was forced to seek employment in order to support himself and his widowed mother. Updike found work for a short period as substitute librarian at the Providence Athenaeum; in 1880 a Boston relative secured him a modest position with the publishing house of Houghton Mifflin. He worked there for the next dozen years in both their Park Street offices and subsequently at their Riverside Press in Cambridge. In those dozen years he graduated from office boy to advertising-copy arranger to full-fledged book designer. Updike took to his new career in printing with reluctance, and it was only with time that he came to embrace his work with increasing interest and understanding.

During the last quarter of the nineteenth century, a new spirit and style, known as the Arts and Crafts movement, emerged in printing as well as in all the arts. The waning years of the Victorian era experienced a deterioration and debasement of artistic design as well as the loss of standards both in Britain and the United States. William Morris of England was the protean moving force during this period, and his example was to prove paramount and irresistible to many designers, including the young Updike.

At the age of thirty-three, Updike decided to leave the safety of the Houghton Mifflin-Riverside Press milieu, where he had never been completely happy, to establish his own business. Calling himself a "Typographic advisor"–it would be several years before Updike's enterprise actually possessed presses of its own–he began working in the mid-summer of 1893. Only two books were printed that first year, one being a small edition of poetry by M. A. De Wolfe Howe. What enabled Updike to attract personalities of Howe's caliber, and to find work in those early days of the Press, was not so much his developing abilities as his family and social connections. But these connections, such as his kinship with the Brown family of Rhode Island, however useful at the beginning, could never have provided Updike with the wherewithal to continue had not the Press produced increasingly distinguished work.

An interesting sidelight in the development of The Merrymount Press was the hiring in 1893 of an Italian immigrant printer, John Bianchi, who ultimately became Updike's only partner. Although they came from totally divergent social backgrounds, the two men complemented each other perfectly. Updike, despite his lack of a university education, became so erudite a practitioner that he not only came to lecture at Harvard, receiving an honorary degree there, but eventually earned the sobriquet of "America's Scholar-Printer." Updike's lectures became the basis for the massive two-volume *Printing Types*, published in 1922 by Harvard University Press, which is considered one of the most scholarly and influential works on the history of printing. The book is still in print today. It was this extraordinary accumulated knowledge that informed Updike's work.

Bianchi, for his part, ran the printing as well as the business side of the Press while earning a law degree through a correspondence course in his spare time. After Updike's death in 1941, Bianchi continued to run the Press until his own retirement in 1949, a retirement which signaled the demise of The Merrymount Press. These two men, one from the established, prominent social class, and the other from the newly-arrived immigrant class, managed to develop and work together for nearly fifty years in the mainstream of the American tradition, making their press not only a symbol of that tradition but also one of the finest in the world.

The name "Merrymount" derived from a wealthy American immigrant of 1628, Thomas Morton, who settled in Wollaston near Quincy, Massachusetts. Morton called his house "Merrymount," where, as legend has it, he put up a maypole to celebrate life, in contravention to his gloomy Puritan neighbors. A young and forward-looking Updike wrote: "We regard Morton's Maypole as a symbol of work done cheerfully and well; of happiness found in work-a-day things; of a high aim and pleasure in trying to attain it." Happiness and cheerfulness were to elude Updike, but of work well done there was abundance.

The bibliography of The Merrymount Press, originally published in 1934, was updated in 1975 to cover the final years of the Press. It lists 1,037 major works and some 1,000 more items considered "minor works." In fact, the Press was responsible for printing over 20,000 items during its fifty-six-year existence. The Huntington Library in San Marino, California, became the main repository of this material when it acquired several collections, including that of Max Farrand's, its first director, and the bulk of the Press's own material after its closing in 1949.

Merrymount's range of printing was extraordinary: bookplates, advertisements, concert programs, catalogues, greeting cards, periodicals, commerical press editions, private fine editions, university, foundation, and government tracts, first editions of literature, musical scores, diplomas, etc. Each work, even those so-called "ephemera" (some of which Updike considered his best work), received professional attention from either Updike or Bianchi. At its largest, the Press never exceeded thirty-five employees, and as Updike wrote: "Over and over again we have said that all kinds of work are done here and no piece of printing, however small, is neglected–much less despised . . . Perhaps the reason I survived—was that a simple idea had got hold of me—to make work better for its purpose than was commonly thought worthwhile."

The literature on The Merrymount Press is extensive, dating from the end of the nineteenth century until the present. As the Press developed, printers here and abroad became aware of its accomplishments, as well as clients for whom fine printing served their own particular ends. Edith Wharton insisted that her publisher, Scribner's, use The Merrymount Press to design and print her books; she understood how a well-designed and well-printed book enhanced a work. Numerous letters in the Wharton-Scribner Archive at Princeton University, and at the Providence Public Library, reflect her appreciation of fine printing and its effect on the literary page.

The lifelong association between Brown University and the Press resulted in works ranging from broadsides and announcements to annual reports to major multivolume bibliographies, the latter in particular underscoring the need for fine, inventive, scholarly printing. Updike's handling of the John Carter Brown Library *Bibliotheca Americana* catalogue (no. 63), with its enormously complex entries, is considered one of the finest examples of catalogue printing ever done in this country.

Both Harvard University and The Grolier Club had occasional business with the Press. Three books were published by the University itself, and ten others by the Harvard University Press—most of those written by Updike himself (nos. 67, 79). Harvard University Press also published the Merrymount bibliography. It should also be noted that books written by faculty and alumni of the University were printed by the Press over the years.

For The Grolier Club, some dozen items were printed from 1911 until 1941. Chief among them was the beautiful three-volume Washington Irving with Rudolph Ruzicka's aquatints heightened with watercolors (no. 66), one of the Press's great productions. In 1921, it sold for $30.00.

.   .   .

THIS EXHIBITION tries to demonstrate in approximately 130 examples (most of which are discussed in the catalogue) the breadth and beauty of the Press's work, and the standard it set for both commercial and fine printing of the day. These examples belong to several distinct periods.

Stylistically, Updike's early period began roughly in 1891 and ended with the century. In this first decade, of which he spent the last seven years on his own, he experimented with a variety of styles and designs. The Arts and Crafts influence can be seen in his choice of borders, decorations, and illustrations, as well as in the considerable use of Old Style and black-letter types. Alternating with that mode was a more chaste approach, and the use of Caslon and Scotch types. Certainly his *Dedication of American Churches* (no. 1) from 1891 is the aesthetic antithesis to the almost overwhelming Arts and Crafts style of *The Altar Book* of 1896 (no. 8). In the first seven years of the Press, some fifty-eight major items were produced, while in just the first two years of the new century, the output was equal to that of the nineties.

The success of the *Dedication of American Churches* led to the decision to produce *The Altar Book*, which was to be financed by Harold Brown. Work commenced on *The Altar Book* in 1893, and it may have been Brown's backing which enabled Updike to begin his own business that same year, despite the fact that the country was then in a financial depression. One can sense a certain unconscious resistance to the Arts and Crafts style, which no matter how competently practiced by Updike, was never congenial to him. The passion which produced *The Altar Book*, and which had generated the Church dedication book of 1891, emanated in large part from Updike's early and fervent religious piety. He brought to these works an intense desire to make them worthy of their sacred subject. Devout his whole life long, Updike handled religious material, especially that for the Episcopal Church of America, with a special understanding and power. *The Altar Book* is the supreme symbol of Updike's nineteenth-century vision as a believer and a printer, just as *The Book of Common Prayer* of 1928 was to be in the next century.

A second period began with the advent of the twentieth century and continued until the First World War. This was an enormously fertile time for Updike and the Press, and by its end Merrymount was established as being capable of the finest printing, comparable to anything produced both here and abroad. From the earliest part of this period come the charming *Selections* (no. 19), the masterly *In the Dawn of the World* (no. 24), the enchanting *Arcady in Troy* (no. 30), and the powerful Tacitus of 1904 (no. 31). A copy of the Tacitus was sent by Mrs. Barrett Wendell to Theodore Roosevelt who, it turned out, was a bibliophile much enamored of and knowledgeable about Venetian fifteenth-century printing. "By George," he wrote back, "it is a pleasure to see such work done in America! . . . What remarkable work Updike is doing. . . . Do you recollect my speaking to you about the remarkable Venetian Fifteenth Century printing; and saying I did not think we had any modern printing that compared with it? Upon my word I think that Updike's Tacitus runs it close."[1] High praise from high places.

During this period, multivolume sets of work by Lamb (no. 20), Cellini (no. 37), and Milton (no. 47), as well as illustrated books of the most sophisticated quality and variety, such as *The Poet Gray as a Naturalist* (no. 25) and Turner's *Liber Studiorum* (no. 56), were printed. An extraordinary undertaking from the editorial, organizational, design, and printing points of view were the two series (in eight volumes) called "The Humanists' Library." Lewis Einstein was the general editor, with individual volumes edited by Roger Fry, J. W. Mackail, and W. A. Bradley, among others. The first volume issued was Maurice Baring's translation of Leonardo da Vinci's *Thoughts on Art and Life* (no. 39). Subsequent volumes such as *Petrarch and the Ancient World* (no. 43) by Pierre de Nolhac, and Sir Philip Sidney's *Defence of Poesie* (no. 45), edited by George Woodberry, appeared in the first series printed between 1906 and 1908. The second series, from 1912 to

1914, included works by Dürer and Pico della Mirandola. Both series were a great critical success; they were textually appealing and superbly designed. T. M. Cleland and W. A. Dwiggins as well as Herbert Horne, who worked on the first series and whose Montallegro type was used throughout, all contributed to making this perhaps the Press's finest achievement in the second period.

The books, pamphlets, and ephemera at this time are highly inventive; the paper, binding, and presswork are often exemplary; and the growing concern with nuance and detail is obvious. Further attention was given to scrupulous editing and proofreading; and an intense, ever-widening awareness of the possibilities of type and decorative arrangement are clearly evident. This period was also a productive time for other printing houses, both here and abroad. The Merrymount Press developed without much heralding during these first two decades, but by the end of the First World War the Press was about to enter into its greatest period—which would come to a glorious end only with the start of the Great Depression.

One superb book after another issued from the Press during these years, bibliographically the midpoint in the Press's life. In 1918, the Press printed the aforementioned *Bibliotheca Americana* (no. 63) for the John Carter Brown Library in an edition of only 250 regular and twenty-five special copies, which has unfortunately limited its availability to the printing enthusiast.

The private commissions for William Bixby (nos. 69, 70, 71, 73) and for the descendants of the Amory family (nos. 74, 75) resulted in books of considerable elegance. The finest paper, bindings, and facsimile illustrations were used. The post-war years were years of prosperity, optimism, and manifest opulence. But as opulent as the times may have been, under Updike, suitability and sensibility precluded ostentation.

The luxurious memento publication, *An Account of the Dedication of the West Window* of a Massachusetts church (no. 83), printed virtually in tandem with a sober but handsome memorial volume for those who served and died in the First World War, *The Public Latin School of Boston* (no. 84), demonstrated the Press's range of expression and taste. But the extraordinary effort put forth by Updike, Bianchi, and the Press in the competition for and the ultimate printing of *The Book of Common Prayer* of 1928 (no. 102) was the culminating work produced from this period. In every way, this book can be seen as Updike's zenith, both spiritually and aesthetically. J. P. Morgan, Jr., in the grand tradition of his father, sponsored and paid for the printing of the revised Standard Book of Common Prayer for the Episcopal Church in America. The story of this many years' endeavor is told elsewhere, but the result of this most assiduous and concentrated period of activity resulted in what is unquestionably the Press's masterwork, and one of the finest pieces of printing ever done in America.

In the decade remaining to Updike, a considerable number of fine books, even superlative ones, issued from the Press. The Great Depression and the concomitant exhaustive and exhausting effort which followed the monumental *Book of Common Prayer* eventually were to take their toll. Updike, in his eighth decade, relaxed, and perhaps for the first time in his life permitted a degree of honor and public retrospection to come his way.

Purged by a physical and also probably psychological illness in the mid-1930s, he spent his last years, active as ever, experimenting with new types and new compositions in his instinctive quest for the perfectly balanced and perfectly printed book.

John Howard Benson's 1940 book, *The Elements of Lettering* (no. 132), Van Wyck Brooks's *The Flowering of New England*, 1941, done for the Limited Editions Club, and Updike's own *Some Aspects of Printing*, also 1941 – which were among the last items designed by Updike – all exhibit a perhaps too conscious effort to be "modern." These books look a little uncomfortable in what never was a ground-breaking *oeuvre*. Next to their more classically conceived bibliographic cousins of those same years, these works appear almost anomalous. There are many Merrymount Press books that, while not self-consciously modern, are not in the least *retardataire*, and could never be mistaken as belonging to any other period.

Once again war had engulfed the world, and several weeks following Pearl Harbor, Updike died after a brief illness, just shy of his eighty-second birthday.

· ·

PERHAPS a celebratory essay should not dwell on the personalities of its principals. Yet it is interesting and illuminating to compare those of Updike and of his partner John Bianchi.

M. A. De Wolfe Howe, who knew Updike probably as well as anyone, commented, "Let it be said at once that he could never have achieved what he did had he not been essentially a perfectionist." Indeed, Updike's family motto could not be more appropriate: "Optimum vix satis," the best is barely enough. "Updike's work," Howe continued, "was so much an expression of his personality that one can hardly be understood without some knowledge of the other. Pretense and compromise were equally foreign to his nature. This was as true of his printing as everything else about him."[2]

Royal Cortissoz also commented on Updike, the man and his work: "The beautiful printing of a book spells character. Is Printing a trade and not an art? How are we to differentiate the elements in a printer's nature? They are not to be divided into watertight compartments. The book, like the painting or the statue, is the product of the whole man. . . . He prints like a great gentleman. An accent of nobility rests upon his art."[3]

Whatever his character, Updike was never a happy man. Very late in life he observed in a letter to T. M. Cleland, "I have not changed much – I often wish I could or had. It is not much fun being 'me.' However, one has one's uses which are not promoted fussing about oneself."[4] In a letter to his friend Edith Wharton he sounded an even darker note:

"When I look ruefully on what I have made of the Press, the aspect is 'rueful' *because* I have not seen life in the round"–devoting as he did all his energies there–"to the detriment of everything else."[5] This sad summation was expressed again in 1940 to the printer Peter Beilenson: "One goes on from day to day doing the best one can–and to my mind that is all there is to it; and a wiser person than myself might have made less of what Miss Amy Lowell once termed 'a dent on one's generation,' and more of life."[6] Yet from this often unhappy, deeply religious, and tormented soul, there came great work.

Daniel Bianchi wrote that his father was always content to remain in the background, and "never found the slightest quarrel with Updike's attempt at domination nor his determination to take the lion's share of credit for the accomplishments of the Press in the eyes of the outside world."[7] Perhaps, in this sense, his father knew best. From all that is known about their forty-eight-year relationship–Updike, the emotional *genius loci*, and Bianchi, the steadfast, practical, and technically proficient practitioner–it seems unlikely that the Press would ever have survived or become as great as it did without the two of them working in concert. Updike needed a Bianchi and Bianchi needed an Updike. As competent a designer and stable a force as Bianchi was, it was Updike who brought great style and historical sensibilities to the Press. For the eight years following Updike's death, Bianchi struggled to keep the Press going–half of those years in the privation of wartime–but the magic was gone.

Obviously, the exhibits cannot hope to cover every aspect of the Press's production, although selections have been made to show the development, range, and most important, the beauty of Merrymount Press printing. Necessarily, the selection is a personal one, and the viewers familiar with the Press's work may look in vain for their favorite item. Every attempt has been made to balance the exhibition, but no attempt has been made to show the occasional clinker, and for that no apologies are offered. It is the intent to put before the public as elegant and handsome an offering of this incomparable Press as possible. There has not been an extensive exhibition of The Merrymount Press in half a century and for too long even the intelligent observer has had to imagine a "typical" Merrymount book. It is therefore hoped that this show will enlighten and inform its viewers.

Some years after Updike's death, Stanley Morison wrote an assessment of Updike and the Press: "Had Updike lived another eight weeks, he would have been 82 years of age, and had completed half a century at the Merrymount Press. His mature works, accomplished after he was 45, had a quality that is rarer than style. He was 50 when he began the series of lectures that formed the basis of *Printing Types*. These two historical volumes, like his practical work, have character. . . . The essential qualities of the work of the Merrymount Press i.e., accurate composition of the text; occasional decoration; proportionate and therefore satisfactory imposition; scrupulous press work; careful folding, sewing and wrapping of the finished product, may be said without exaggeration or disrespect to De Vinne to have reached a higher degree of quality and consistency than that of any other printing-house of its size, and period of operation, in America or Europe."[8]

A new world and a new outlook began in the post-Second World War years in every aspect of life including necessarily the world of printing. It was for other printers and designers to provide their version of this new world. The Merrymount Press had had its day, nay, its half-century, and glorious it was.

NOTES

1. Theodore Roosevelt, TLS, [White House stationery], Oyster Bay, New York, 30 July 1907, to Mrs. Wendell Barrett. Quoted by kind permission, Special Collections, Providence Public Library.

2. M. A. De Wolfe Howe, "Updike of Merrymount, The Scholar Printer." Reprinted in *Updike: American Printer and His Merrymount Press*, edited by Peter Beilenson (New York: The American Institute of Graphic Arts, 1947), pp. 86 and 90.

3. Royal Cortissoz, "Address by Royal Cortissoz," in *Daniel Berkeley Updike and the Merrymount Press* (New York: The American Institute of Graphic Arts, 1940), p. 12f.

4. T. M. Cleland, "A Tribute to Daniel Berkeley Updike, First Printer." Reprinted in *Updike: American Printer and His Merrymount Press*, edited by Peter Beilenson (New York: The American Institute of Graphic Arts, 1947), p. 85.

5. D. B. Updike, ALS, 338 Marlborough St., Boston, 31 May 1937, to Edith Wharton. Quoted by kind permission, Yale Collection of American Literature, Beinecke Rare Book and Manuscript Library, Yale University.

6. D. B. Updike, TLS, The Merrymount Press, Boston, 17 April 1940, to Peter Beilenson. Quoted by kind permission, Special Collections, Providence Public Library.

7. Daniel B. Bianchi, *D. B. Updike & John Bianchi: A Note on Their Association* (Boston: The Society of Printers, 1965), p. 10.

8. Stanley Morison, "Recollections and Perspectives." Reprinted in *Updike: American Printer and His Merrymount Press*, edited by Peter Beilenson (New York: The American Institute of Graphic Arts, 1947), p. 66.

An incidental difficulty, and one that still interferes with a wider acceptance of Updike's attainment, is in the fact that very few persons, perhaps nobody except his foreman and possibly those who examine a California collection, has seen enough of the Merrymount product to justify passing an expert opinion upon it.

GEORGE PARKER WINSHIP

Daniel Berkeley Updike and the Merrymount Press
Rochester, 1947, page 99

NOTE

All D. B. Updike quotations cited, unless otherwise noted, are from his *Notes on the Merrymount Press and Its Work* contained in Julian Pearce Smith's *Bibliographical List of Books Printed at the Press 1893-1933*, published by Harvard University Press in 1934. When appropriate, each entry has the corresponding SMITH number. Edition sizes are included where known.

CATALOGUE

. .

1. ON THE DEDICATION OF AMERICAN CHURCHES, AN ENQUIRY
INTO THE NAMING OF CHURCHES IN THE UNITED STATES, SOME
ACCOUNT OF ENGLISH DEDICATIONS, AND SUGGESTIONS FOR
FUTURE DEDICATIONS IN THE AMERICAN CHURCH, COMPILED BY
TWO LAYMEN OF THE DIOCESE OF RHODE ISLAND
¶ CAMBRIDGE, PRINTED AT THE RIVERSIDE PRESS, 1891

This book, Updike's first independent work completed while he was still employed at The
Riverside Press, was published jointly by Harold Brown and himself. Its subject, the Episcopal Church, became one of Updike's major printing interests.

The Dedication is carefully designed; its charts and lists already demonstrate Updike's skill
in composing and designing complicated material. The use of black-letter, Franklin Old
Style, and the title-page and colophon design also reflect Updike's antiquarian interest and in-
cipient typographical knowledge. The book created a major stir in ecclesiastical circles, and
led to his commission for the decoration of *The Book of Common Prayer* of 1892 (no. 3).

2. A DAY AT LAGUERRE'S AND OTHER DAYS, NINE SKETCHES BY
F. HOPKINSON SMITH
¶ BOSTON AND NEW YORK, HOUGHTON MIFFLIN AND COMPANY,
THE RIVERSIDE PRESS, CAMBRIDGE, 1892
(LARGE PAPER EDITION, 250 COPIES)

Published a year after *The Dedication of American Churches*, Laguerre's is the only title which
Updike mentions as having been designed by him for Houghton Mifflin while still at Riverside. Its borders, by Harold Van Buren Magonigle, incorporating Walter Crane's Houghton Mifflin publishing emblem, are in the Arts and Crafts style, a style which is used here
by Updike for the first time. The contrasting red printed title is effective, and the design as
a whole, in its modest way, anticipates the full-blown borders of Bertram Goodhue in the
revised *Book of Common Prayer* (no. 3).

3. THE BOOK OF COMMON PRAYER ACCORDING TO THE USE OF THE
PROTESTANT EPISCOPAL CHURCH IN THE UNITED STATES
OF AMERICA
¶ NEW YORK, PRINTED FOR THE COMMITTEE, 1893

The story of Updike's reluctant agreement to arrange the decoration to be added to *The
Book of Common Prayer* of 1892, a first edition which had already been printed by Theodore
De Vinne, is well known. Bertram Grosvenor Goodhue's decorated letters and borders for
the 1893 edition are highly varied and not uninteresting, but they do not in any way inte-
grate or properly complement the text. This integration would come in 1896 with the
printing of *The Altar Book*. Despite the prayer book's shortcomings, it contributed signifi-

cantly to Updike's reputation at a crucial time: when he was about to begin his independent Merrymount Press.

4. VEXILLA REGIS QUOTIDIE, BY L.B.S. [LUCY BRADLEE STONE]
¶ BOSTON, PRIVATELY PRINTED, 1893 (100 COPIES)

Vexilla Regis is Updike's first book as an independent designer on his own. He had no presses at this point nor had he employed the name Merrymount, but *Vexilla Regis* is considered, bibliographically, the first. The book is simple, balanced, and restrained. It is rubricated with a discreet use of black-letter; the text has inspiring quotations for each month of the year. Printed at The Riverside Press, *Vexilla* is an appropriate and modest beginning to a corpus of over 20,000 works. It is highly significant as well as symbolic that Updike's first Merrymount book should be pietistic.

SMITH I

5. BILL PRATT/THE SAW-BUCK PHILOSOPHER, BY JOHN SHERIDAN ZELIE
¶ WILLIAMSTOWN, 1895

Bill Pratt displays Updike's second use of Caslon, a typeface he favored throughout the years. The design is self-assured and the border seems to anticipate Art Nouveau in its gentle rather than heavily medievalized way. Updike indulged in much experimentation with the Arts and Crafts style during this early period.

SMITH 13

6. THE GOVERNOR'S GARDEN
¶ BOSTON, GEORGE R. R. RIVERS, JOSEPH KNIGHT CO., 1896

In 1896, Updike moved his office around the corner from Beacon Street to Tremont Place. He issued a memorial service for Martin Brimmer, the first work to appear with "The Merrymount Press" imprint. However, it was his next book, *The Governor's Garden*, which was actually the first one set at the Press with a small amount of recently purchased type. It was designed by the then foreman, John Bianchi. Conscious effort was made to create an American colonial flavor by using various Caslon type units in the borders and headpieces.

SMITH 17

7. THE NIGHTINGALE, BY HANS CHRISTIAN ANDERSEN
¶ BOSTON, BERKELEY UPDIKE, THE MERRYMOUNT PRESS, 1896

The Nightingale is the second of the very few books published by Updike; it employs Japanese-fold pages, a device likewise rarely used by him. The title-page design and the four illustrations are by Mary Newill of the then popular Birmingham Guild of Handicraft. One senses here a conscious attempt to find interesting type and decorative arrangements.

SMITH 19

8. THE ALTAR BOOK: CONTAINING THE ORDER FOR THE EUCHARIST ACCORDING TO THE USE OF THE AMERICAN CHURCH
¶ 1896 (350 COPIES)

Following the death of William Morris, Updike made a pilgrimage to Kelmscott House. Like many other printers in Europe and America, he was initially infatuated with the Arts and Crafts style. Only once, however, did this style emerge full-blown: in his *Altar Book* of 1896.

The Altar Book was three years in the making. With the financial help of Harold Brown, Updike was able to give full reign to his typographical ideas and ecclesiastical knowledge.

This book represents a high point in the American Arts and Crafts bookmaking style. The type, dubbed "Merrymount," was commissioned from Bertram Grosvenor Goodhue, who also drew the borders and initials, of which no two are alike. There is certainly a far better integration of borders and text here than in those for *The Book of Common Prayer* of 1892-93. And yet these borders, as splendid as they are, compete with Richard Anning Bell's illustrations—perhaps because they both are so strong and from separate hands. However, Goodhue's magnificent pigskin binding is a beautiful late nineteenth-century American example.

The Press's facilities proved inadequate for production of this book, and special rooms had to be rented elsewhere. The actual printing of the work was left to De Vinne in New York, who executed near flawless presswork on specially ordered handmade paper.

The Kelmscott *Chaucer* appeared some months after *The Altar Book*. Although both books were magnificent, they soon became stylistic anachronisms. But their sumptuousness and craftsmanship excited the book world, and their influence was felt for years. In truth, the Arts and Crafts style was incompatible with Updike's more restrained aesthetic sensibility. But he, like most of the printers and designers of the 1890s, had to pass through this artistically fertile period in order to find his own way. Several years after publication, St. John Hornby wrote Updike that his *Altar Book* was as "good as anything since the Kelmscott Press was at work."*

*St. John Hornby, ALS, Shelley House, Chelsea, London, S.W., to D. B. Updike, 11 September 1907. Quoted by kind permission, Special Collections, Providence Public Library.

SMITH 20

9. WHAT IS WORTHWHILE? BY ANNA ROBERTSON BROWN
¶ NEW YORK AND BOSTON, THOMAS Y. CROWELL AND COMPANY, 1897

Appearing almost immediately after *The Altar Book*, this small volume printed in Clarendon type has decorations by Bertram Goodhue. He also designed the cover and title-page, both of which harmonize with Updike's general typography. There is a quiet, subdued unity here unlike the stylistic fortissimo of the preceding book. *What is Worthwhile?* was the first work Updike printed for Thomas Crowell and Company of New York, a firm whose patronage during the early years of the Press was welcomed. These books have a certain turn-of-the-century appeal, and are, in fact, respectable commercial products.

SMITH 22

10. THE DECORATION OF HOUSES, BY EDITH WHARTON AND
OGDEN CODMAN, JR.
¶ NEW YORK, CHARLES SCRIBNER'S SONS, 1897

Updike's friendship with Edith Wharton led to the early commission of her first book at Scribner's. This celebrated decorating treatise boasts a cover and title-page design by Updike; it was not printed at The Merrymount Press but rather by De Vinne (hence not catalogued as a Merrymount Press book.) The title-page with an architectural frame was a device Updike clearly liked. He employed various permutations of decorative frames for title-pages during the next decade.

11. ALICE IN WONDERLAND, A PLAY COMPILED FROM LEWIS
CARROLL'S STORIES
¶ NEW YORK, DODD MEAD & CO., 1898

Updike relied a good deal on Bertram Goodhue's artistic invention during the first decade of the Press—especially in cover design, illustrations, and endpapers. The two men worked well together, and often Updike allowed designers and artists like T. M. Cleland and W. A. Dwiggins to create both cover and title-page designs, albeit under his own guidance. Although many Merrymount Press books are without decoration, there are exceptions, and when the contents of a book dictated decoration, nothing was ever gratuitous. In time, as Updike grew in experience, he felt more comfortable and assured; and while he was always scrupulous in "advising" others, he grew more creative as the years progressed, using freelance designers less frequently.

SMITH 30

12. SHIPS AND HAVENS, BY HENRY VAN DYKE
¶ NEW YORK AND BOSTON, T. Y. CROWELL AND COMPANY, 1898

Another Goodhue cover and title-page design, printed here in Clarendon type and rubricated throughout. The imprint is now Chestnut Street, Boston, where the Press moved in 1898. It continued to expand, and during the next five years took over the building next door. Updike lived over the shop, as it were, on Chestnut Street in rooms arranged by his architect friend Ogden Codman, co-author with Edith Wharton of *The Decoration of Houses* (no. 10), who also was one of America's earliest interior decorators.

SMITH 35

13. A LETTER BOOK WRITTEN 1743–1751, BY THE REVD. JAMES
MACSPARRAN
¶ BOSTON, D. B. UPDIKE, THE MERRYMOUNT PRESS, 1899

"In 1899 appeared under my imprint a book that had a family interest, namely, a diary kept by my great-great-uncle, James MacSparran, D.D., between the years 1743 and 1751. MacSparran was our Anglican missionary sent to Rhode Island by the Venerable Society for the Propagation of the Gospel in Foreign Parts. There he became rector of St. Paul's

Narragansett. His diary is a quaint affair recording the daily life of an American Parson Woodforde. In printing it I conformed to the manuscript—superior letters, odd spelling, and all." So Updike describes the work of his ancestor, appropriately printed in Caslon in a "period" setting. Books such as this became staples of the Press.

SMITH 38

14. THE GREATER INCLINATION, BY EDITH WHARTON
¶ NEW YORK, CHARLES SCRIBNER'S SONS, 1899

Edith Wharton held strict ideas on typography, and stipulated that her publisher, Scribner's, employ The Merrymount Press to design and print a number of her books. She met Updike socially—their friendship lasted until her death in 1937—and admired his work. The Wharton letters in the Scribner Archive at Princeton, and several at Providence, give testimony to her involvement in the design, decoration, typography, and binding of each of her books.

The type used here, her first full-length novel, and in all her subsequent books printed by the Press, was Scotch-face. Although it was a typeface used widely in England, Updike was the first in America to employ it in works of fiction. There is no bibliographic indication for the source of the cover and title-page decoration, although it is, in fact, derived from designs by Du Cerceau. There are extant working albums of Du Cerceau and Pillement designs in a private collection that once belonged to T. M. Cleland—sources which Cleland drew heavily upon for his designs at The Merrymount Press. It might be tempting to assume Cleland's hand in several of the works from this year and the next, especially Wharton's *The Touchstone*, which Updike printed in 1900. But it does not appear that Cleland was employed by Updike before 1903, after his move to Boston. Cleland, however, knew Updike earlier—during the course of his own ill-fated independent printing venture, The Cornhill Press, which managed but three books before closing in 1902. It seems more likely that Updike, mentor to the fledgling designer, introduced Cleland to Du Cerceau's Renaissance ornaments and to Pillement's delightful Rococo chinoiseries.

SMITH 49

15. A DESCRIPTION OF THE PASTORAL STAFF GIVEN TO THE DIOCESE OF ALBANY
¶ NEW YORK, 1900 (150 COPIES)

Updike refers to this as a "most ambitious book." It is a costly and highly elaborate commemoration of the pastoral staff given to the Albany diocese and commissioned by its wealthy donor, Mrs. J.V.L. Pruyn. The illustrations are in photogravure which, as Updike points out, "made an odd alliance with a text set throughout in black-letter type." Goodhue designed the grandiose decorations, the opening pages, and the binding. There seems to be very little Updike here. This was, in fact, the Press's last blast of gothicizing Arts and Crafts style, far more congenial now to the church architect Goodhue than to Updike. In an adroit disclaimer, Updike wrote: "The book is an exhibition of his cleverness as a draughtsman rather than of any skill of mine."

SMITH 59

16. THE PRINCE WHO DID NOT EXIST, BY EDWARD PERRY WARREN,
WITH PICTURES BY ARTHUR J. GASKIN
¶ 1900 (350 COPIES)

This small Japanese-fold volume, printed in Caslon "black-letter," provides a vivid contrast to the *Pastoral Staff*. Black-letter, used to medieval effect there, is equally suited to the fairy-tale text here. There is freshness in the typography as well as clarity and openness. Nothing is old-fashioned about the design; and taken together the two books show the best—as here—and the worst tendencies of the Arts and Crafts movement.

SMITH 66

17. RELIGION IN LITERATURE, BY STOPFORD A. BROOKE
¶ NEW YORK, THOMAS Y. CROWELL AND COMPANY, 1901

In the early years of the Press, a number of small volumes such as this one were designed for the firm of Thomas Crowell. Care was always taken to avoid a static formula. Here the richly rubricated decorative title-page provides interest without excess.

SMITH 86

18. THE UNFOLDING LIFE, PASSAGES FROM DIARIES, NOTEBOOKS AND
LETTERS [TO AND FROM] HOWARD MUNRO LONGYEAR
¶ BOSTON, PRIVATELY PRINTED BY THE MERRYMOUNT PRESS,
1901

The Unfolding Life was printed with two different title-pages, one having an illustration by Mary Newill of the Birmingham Guild of Handicraft. The typeface is Caslon. A large paper edition on Japan paper was also printed the following year, in an edition of twenty, with Newill's title-page. For a time, The Merrymount Press was the American agent for the Guild's magazine, *The Quill*, but like so many artistic and intellectual periodicals of the nineties, it proved a fragile enterprise and barely lived to see the century out.

SMITH 100

19. SELECTIONS, KATHARINE COOLIDGE
¶ BOSTON, PRIVATELY PRINTED AT THE MERRYMOUNT PRESS,
1901

Increasingly, members of the well-heeled New England aristocracy began to seek out Updike for printing personal works, family histories, literary vignettes, and the like, which they knew would be discreetly and handsomely treated. These works were often costly productions, as this volume with its vellum spine and corners, paste-paper cover, leather label, and beautiful handmade text paper demonstrates. As Winship points out, the private nature of these works, and their very limited edition size, prevented the public at large from seeing them; and Updike's reputation has never been properly balanced due to a lack of familiarity with these uncommon, privately printed works.

SMITH 105

20. THE LIFE AND WORKS OF CHARLES LAMB
¶ TROY, NEW YORK, PAFRAETS BOOK COMPANY, 1902
(1,000 COPIES)

In 1902, The Merrymount Press printed this twelve-volume edition (12,000 volumes in all) for the Pafraets Book Company. It was a considerable undertaking for the small firm at the time; excepting a fifteen-volume Bible and a handful of three-, four-, or six-volume sets over the years, the Press rarely undertook such large projects. Two-volume sets were more the rule, and huge editions in general did not come their way often. Nevertheless, the multi-volume work received the same care as if smaller, and the "Lamb," in this case, has not been sacrificed to formula because of size.

SMITH 150

21. LITTLE STORIES, BY S. WEIR MITCHELL
¶ NEW YORK, THE CENTURY CO., 1903

From cover to colophon, this book of short stories by S. Weir Mitchell for the Century Company is a complete delight. Many such small volumes were printed during the Press's existence, each just right for its size and contents. There must have been a decided vogue for small books during the first half of this century; today, however, they are the exception.

SMITH 161

22. MORS ET VICTORIA
¶ NEW YORK AND BOMBAY, LONGMANS, GREEN & CO., 1903

There is a restrained use of Renaissance decoration on the spine and title-page, giving a light elegance to this slim volume. Over the years, the Press acquired an extensive complement of borders, cuts, and type decorations. European as well as American designs were frequently adapted from etchings, engravings, book decorations, and period bindings. Beginning as the Press did in the 1890s, the initial emphasis was heavily medieval, then lightened into early and late Renaissance conceits. With time and with a sureness of touch, Updike would ultimately dispense with heavy use of decoration, and rely more on his typography to convey his style.

SMITH 162

23. THE ORDER OF EVENING WORSHIP IN THE MEETING HOUSE ON STAR ISLAND
¶ 1903 (500 COPIES)

The subject of this book is as interesting as its typography. The anchor decoration is suggestive of the sea-setting of the stone meeting house on Star Island in the Isles of Shoals off the Maine coast. This island, which became part of a Unitarian camp, began as an early American resort under the aegis of the father of the American writer Celia Thaxter. To this day there are services in its unchanging, timeless setting. The text type, which at first seems overly large, was set that way because the services were conducted, then as now, by candle-light at sunset.

SMITH 163

24. IN THE DAWN OF THE WORLD, TWENTY-FIVE PICTURES OF THE BOOK OF GENESIS, BY EDWARD BURNE-JONES ¶ BOSTON, CHARLES E. GOODSPEED, 1903 (185 COPIES)

The twenty-five illustrations reproduced in this book were part of a Kelmscott Press project, never completed owing to the death of William Morris. The drawings, originally designed for a large quarto *Biblia Innocentum*, have been cut here by Catterson-Smith on wood, and reproduced for the first time in America. An English edition printed by the Chiswick Press a year earlier was less successful. The character of Goodhue's type is a better complement to the pictures than Chiswick's use of nineteenth-century Old Style. The Merrymount type is used for only the second time since the 1896 *Altar Book*, but how different is its effect under Updike's ever more masterful hand. There are no elaborate borders to distract from either the Burne-Jones cuts or the superb printing of the *mise-en-page*. Updike has balanced the English and the more concise Latin text with great skill. By now the stylistic influence of Morris is gone, and an approach closer to that of the Doves Press is apparent.

SMITH 169

25. THE POET GRAY AS A NATURALIST, BY CHARLES ELIOT NORTON ¶ BOSTON, CHARLES E. GOODSPEED, 1903 (500 COPIES)

In 1901, The Merrymount Press began an association with Charles Goodspeed and Company which continued throughout the life of the Press. It printed books, pamphlets, broadsides, catalogues, greeting cards, and the like for Goodspeed's. This book from 1903 is particularly fine—printed on handmade paper with facsimiles of Gray's drawings. One senses Updike very much in his stride with a near perfect combination of typography, illustration, and binding. A period of transition for the Press, beginning around 1901 and continuing until 1904, is discernable.

SMITH 170

26. THE PERSONALITY OF EMERSON, BY F. B. SANBORN ¶ BOSTON, CHARLES E. GOODSPEED, 1903 (500 COPIES)

More typical of the books done for Goodspeed is this essay on Emerson, as elegant in its simplicity and as beautifully printed as anything Updike and the Press ever did during their early years. There is a clarity and precision that is particularly appealing, which today seems as American as its subject.

SMITH 174

27. THE POEMS OF DANTE GABRIEL ROSSETTI
¶ TROY, NEW YORK, THE PAFRAETS BOOK COMPANY, 1903
(500 COPIES)

The two-volume Cheyne Walk Edition of Rossetti's complete poems was arranged and edited by Herbert Copeland, who had been a partner in the distinguished–if short lived–publishing firm of Copeland and Day in Boston. The cover and title-page have designs by T. M. Cleland. This elegant set is beautifully printed on Arnold handmade paper, and exhibits a confident and refined style.

SMITH 177

28. THE LIFE OF MICHELAGNOLO BUONARROTI, COLLECTED BY ASCANIO CONDIVI
¶ BOSTON, 1904

Herbert Horne was commissioned by Updike to create a new type called Montallegro, a roman letter modeled on early Florentine fonts. Horne insisted on designing the first book set in his type, choosing the square format of Florentine woodcut books. Bernard Berenson wrote Updike complimenting him on the new type: "I certainly know of no type since Aldus that pleases me so well: and in some respect, as for instance in its lapidary and cursive character, I am not sure that it does not even surpass Aldus."* Updike, however, was never entirely satisfied with Montallegro, which he felt was too rigid and self-conscious, and in this work more solidly set than he would have done. Nevertheless, the work has a certain period appeal.

*Bernhard Berenson, ALS, I Tatti, Settignano, Florence, 20 January 1902, to D. B. Updike. Quoted by kind permission, Special Collections, Providence Public Library.

SMITH 189

29. SARAH WHITMAN
¶ BOSTON, THE MERRYMOUNT PRESS, 1903

Sarah Wyman Whitman was a highly active artist living in Boston. She painted, designed jewelry, church decorations, stained-glass windows, and most importantly, books for Houghton Mifflin in her very handsome and highly distinctive style. Her designs were used occasionally by Updike, as here in her own memorial volume. Whitman was part of a group of independent designers, artists, and editors living in the Boston area to whom the Press gave frequent commissions. However, Updike had no hesitation in using the occasional free-lance designer from other places, including Europe.

SMITH 195

30. ARCADY IN TROY
¶ BOSTON, THE MERRYMOUNT PRESS, 1904

This captivating book has a title-page decoration by T. M. Cleland. There are two slight variants of this design, an indication of the care with which even the smallest details were regarded by the Press. In one version the fountain lacks its dark green pool of water, and the ink is of a different hue. The Troy here is, surprisingly, the one in New York State, and the subject of the book concerns a wildflower garden in the midst of that city.

SMITH 201

31. CORNELII TACITI, DE VITA ET MORIBUS IULII AGRICOLAE
¶ BOSTON, THE MERRYMOUNT PRESS, 1904 (100 COPIES)

One of the largest and in many ways the most majestic book printed at The Merrymount Press, this *opera minora* of Tacitus was undertaken at the suggestion of Charles Eliot Norton. It was edited by Professor Morris H. Morgan of Harvard. Updike sent sample pages of his Tacitus abroad, maintaining that "our choice of this text suggested its use to the Doves Press." There is considerable evidence, in letters sent back and forth across the Atlantic, of the exchange of printed material between The Merrymount Press and English presses of the day. By this time the influence was no longer going in one direction. The cover has gold-stamped letters designed by Sarah Whitman, with the text printed in Goodhue's Merrymount—a rare use of it by the Press—and it has never looked better than here on large unadorned pages. The colophon, in Latin, reads in part, ". . . Magister Daniel Berkeley Updike in officina sua quae Hilarimontium dicitur. . . ."

SMITH 202

32. A BOOK OF BEVERAGES
¶ WORCESTER, MASSACHUSETTS, BIGELOW CHAPTER, DAUGHTERS OF THE AMERICAN REVOLUTION, 1904

The colonial-style format of this book on early American beverages is well suited to the subject and no doubt pleased its patrons, the Daughters of the American Revolution. The subtitle reads: ". . . Recipes secured from those Housewives most Notable for their Skill in the Preparation of Choice & Delectable Beverages for Winter Nights and Summer Noons."

SMITH 203

33. A NOTABLE LIBEL CASE, BY JOSIAH H. BENTON, JR.
¶ BOSTON, CHARLES E. GOODSPEED, 1904 (400 COPIES)

By this time, the format of American books being printed for Charles Goodspeed and Company was changing. The attractive design used for Sanborn's hagiographical books on Thoreau and Emerson were no longer appropriate for the subject of this volume—a law case prosecuted by Daniel Webster in 1828.

SMITH 207

34. AN EMPTY PURSE, A CHRISTMAS STORY, BY SARAH ORNE JEWETT
¶ PRIVATELY PRINTED, 1905

This rare and pleasing pamphlet of Jewett's short story was printed in Scotch-face, a type Updike favored for fiction. Many of Jewett's books, published by Houghton Mifflin, were designed by Sarah Wyman Whitman, who died in 1904. *An Empty Purse* was originally published in 1895, and is here reprinted by Updike for a charitable benefit sale at Jewett's request.

SMITH 212

35. THE MARCHING MORROWS
¶ BOSTON, THE WOMEN'S EDUCATIONAL AND INDUSTRIAL UNION, 1905

The Marching Morrows is an example of an inexpensively printed volume for which care was taken with text, title-page, and printed-paper-over-boards cover. Updike was always experimenting, and no job was ever considered too pedestrian for finding an appropriate and felicitous design.

SMITH 218

36. THE SCHOOL OF LIFE, BY HENRY VAN DYKE
¶ NEW YORK, CHARLES SCRIBNER'S SONS, 1905

In many ways this little volume is typical of a large number of similar books printed at the Press. Usually bound in paper over boards with a cloth spine, with or without a spine label, these slim volumes are often considered "typical" Merrymount Press books. Although many of them appear similar at first, each bears its own special stamp of distinction, as in the delightful, unassuming title-page of this work.

SMITH 221

37. THE LIFE OF BENVENUTO CELLINI, EDITED AND TRANSLATED BY JOHN ADDINGTON SYMONDS, WITH REPRODUCTIONS OF PORTRAITS AND VIEWS
¶ NEW YORK, BRENTANO'S, 1906

The title-page of this two-volume life of Cellini was designed by T. M. Cleland. The binding was designed by Laurence Housman, and the typeface used is Mountjoye. The edition had great success and was subsequently reprinted, but not by Merrymount, and never as well. These books were meant to be read, and like so many books printed at the Press, were eminently readable: they rest easily in the hand.

SMITH 239

38. GREAT RICHES, BY CHARLES W. ELIOT, PRESIDENT OF HARVARD UNIVERSITY
¶ NEW YORK, THOMAS Y. CROWELL & CO., 1906

During the early days of the Press, many books like *Great Riches* were farmed out: composition and electrotype plates were done at the Press but the printing was executed elsewhere—and never as well as the Press would have done. Winship maintains that sometimes books were sent out for printing in order to avoid a major back-up at the Press. This was particularly true for large editions, especially in the early years.

SMITH 240

39. THOUGHTS ON ART AND LIFE BY LEONARDO DA VINCI,
TRANSLATED BY MAURICE BARING
¶ BOSTON, THE MERRYMOUNT PRESS, 1906 (303 COPIES)

This is the first volume in a series known as "The Humanists' Library." Various designers were commissioned to do the elegant decorations. In this volume the artist is Herbert Horne, whose Montallegro type is used to better advantage than before. The first series consisted of four volumes in 303 copies. "The Humanists' Library" was a success, and hailed in literary as well as design circles. A second series was issued in 1912–1913, with an additional four volumes in much the same format, although the price of the volumes was halved in an attempt to reach a larger book-reading public. The lowered price failed to attract new subscribers: it was felt that the lesser price implied a lesser book. A lesson, perhaps, in book snobbery.

SMITH 247

40. HISTORIE OF SIR WILLIAM KIRKALDY, KNIGHT
¶ BOSTON, THE CLUB OF ODD VOLUMES, 1906 (114 COPIES)

The *Historie*, printed on Arnold handmade paper, is not atypical of small editions printed for the Club of Odd Volumes, a Boston book club, many of whose members had professional, social, or family connections to Updike. Much of the printing Merrymount did for them, including books, invitations, menus, and the like, was executed with considerable charm. The Club of Odd Volumes ephemera—which runs into the hundreds—is some of the most delightful work by the Press. There is sophistication and wit in much of the Odd Volumes' work. The Press began printing for the Club in 1904, but the *Historie* was the first full-scale commission.

SMITH 258

41. THE DUTIES & QUALIFICATIONS OF A LIBRARIAN, BY JEAN-
BAPTISTE COTTON DES HOUSSAYES
¶ CHICAGO, A. C. MCCLURG & CO., 1906 (250 COPIES)

The six little volumes of the *Literature of Library* series, edited by John Cotton Dana and Henry Watson Kent, contain essays on libraries of the seventeenth and eighteenth centuries. They were printed in a regular edition of only 250 copies, and a large paper edition of twenty-five. Each of the volumes had an extra decorative title-page printed in black and brown. The type is Mountjoye.

SMITH 259

42. THE FIRST BOOK OF THE DOFOBS
¶ CHICAGO, PRINTED FOR THE SOCIETY OF THE DOFOBS, 1907
(50 COPIES)

This small edition for the Chicago Book Society of the Dofobs (so named after the Roman bibliophile Dofobius) is half-bound in vellum with a leather label, and has an illustration by Howard Pyle as frontispiece. Mountjoye type is printed on particularly fine Italian handmade paper. The binding and paper combine with a rubricated decorative title-page to make this a splendid Merrymount volume.

SMITH 278

43. PETRARCH AND THE ANCIENT WORLD, BY PIERRE DE NOLHAC
¶ 1907 (303 COPIES)

The rich rubricated title-page and decorative initials as well as the text settings of Mont-allegro type printed with marginal notes make a handsome page in this third volume of the Humanists' series. Each title-page in the series varies, having been commissioned from a different designer. Edith Wharton had hoped to write an introduction to one of the volumes but nothing came of it as she felt unqualified to write about the subject proposed. She did, however, subscribe enthusiastically to the series, which has remained popular with collectors today.

SMITH 286

44. THREE PROCLAMATIONS CONCERNING THE LOTTERY FOR
VIRGINIA, 1613–1621
¶ PROVIDENCE, RHODE ISLAND, THE JOHN CARTER BROWN
LIBRARY, 1907 (100 COPIES)

The Merrymount Press did few folio size volumes. Large size for large size sake would have been anathema to the conservative Updike. However, in this case the large size facsimiles of the proclamation required a folio, and Updike responded by creating a strong and generous title-page. The facsimile reproductions are beautifully executed, and the printing is flawless. Merrymount type makes a rare appearance here. Updike felt it was only suited for large books—in fact, he used it only twice after this project. The Merrymount Press had begun printing for Brown University and its libraries in 1905, and their association continued for over four decades.

SMITH 288

45. THE DEFENCE OF POESIE, A LETTER TO Q. ELIZABETH, A
DEFENCE OF LEICESTER, BY SIR PHILIP SIDNEY, EDITED BY
G. E. WOODBERRY
¶ BOSTON, THE MERRYMOUNT PRESS, 1908 (303 COPIES)

The fourth volume of "The Humanists' Library" first series has a title-page by W. A. Dwiggins with initials and colophon by Herbert Horne. The eight volumes in two series were separately edited or translated by such authorities as Maurice Baring and Roger Fry. All the volumes in both series were under the general editorship of Lewis Einstein.

SMITH 302

46. CARCASSONE, GUSTAVE NADAUD, JULIA C. R. DORR
¶ PRIVATELY PRINTED, CHRISTMAS, 1908 (75 COPIES)

A small, privately printed volume of translated French poetry (for Thomas Nast Fairbanks) most attractively bound in Italian decorated paper. Updike often paid special attention to binding. In the early years, while travelling abroad, he would buy small quantities of antique papers to use at the Press. If there were sufficient funds at his disposal for a particular edition, he would commission special endpapers as well as designs for covers or spines. At the very least, bindings by the Press were neat and simple, often with a cloth spine, printed paper label, and good quality paper over boards. In the first years of the Press, Updike employed the services of J. E. Hill, who occupied an adjacent office; it was he who supplied ornaments for the work of the Press. Updike frequently used a gray-blue paper for covers which, he wrote, reminded him of the "Seidlitz" medicinal powder wrappers of his youth. The smallest detail of binding might have to be pondered over for a client. For one such client, Sarah Cooper Hewitt, Updike chose "Empire paper, with white label, yellow edges, and end-papers printed from wood-blocks in green and pink. . . . The book-marker in blue and pink was much consulted about, and Miss Hewitt . . . adjured me that under no possible pretence should like end-papers and ribbons adorn the books of one other living being!"

SMITH 317

47. THE POETICAL WORKS OF JOHN MILTON, WITH A LIFE OF THE AUTHOR, AND ILLUSTRATIONS
¶ BOSTON, R. H. HINKLEY COMPANY, 1908 (555 COPIES)

The poetry of Milton in four half-leather bound volumes has title-page and decorations by W. A. Dwiggins. The illustrations are adapted from Flaxman and printed in sepia. The use of Mountjoye type is particularly effective here, and the impression on specially handmade paper is crisp and satisfying. The introductory texts to Milton's English and Latin verse are both invitingly readable.

SMITH 319

48. READING A POEM BY WM. MAKEPEACE THACKERAY
¶ NEW YORK, THE GROLIER CLUB, 1911 (250 COPIES)

Reading a Poem contains sketches by Thackeray "redrawn" by W. A. Dwiggins, who also designed the title-page and colophon. The body of the text is printed in an unusually small size Scotch-face type not often employed by the Press. Updike printed seven major books for The Grolier Club in New York, of which this was the first.

SMITH 353

49. ARCHIVES OF THE GENERAL CONVENTION, THE CORRESPONDENCE OF JOHN HENRY HOBART [1757–1811]
¶ NEW YORK, PRIVATELY PRINTED, 1911 [1912] (250 COPIES)

Discussing these archives of the Episcopal Church, Updike wrote: "An important work printed in six volumes in 1911, at the expense of the late Mr. J. Pierpont Morgan. . . . It was intended to issue more volumes, but the Hobart correspondence was so interminably strung out by the editor and the prospect of arriving at the end of the series became so remote that the project was given up. These severely plain volumes were set in Mountjoye type combined with those Oxford founts which accord well with it."

Despite the problems Updike had with the editor, J. P. Morgan, Jr. and Belle Da Costa Greene were enormously pleased with the result of this second Morgan project–the first being the improved decorations for *The Book of Common Prayer* of 1892–93. Their pleasure proved of great importance to Updike in the coming years.

SMITH 355

50. LETTERS OF BULWER-LYTTON TO MACREADY, WITH AN INTRODUCTION BY BRANDER MATTHEWS
¶ NEWARK, NEW JERSEY, THE CARTERET BOOK CLUB, 1911 (100 COPIES)

Updike calls this handsome book a "period" volume. Clearly the Press attempted to evoke an antiquarian aura when dealing with certain texts of an earlier period. Indeed, such attempts were fashionable at the time, and no one else in America did them as well, with the exception of Bruce Rogers. Both Updike and Rogers, however, were criticized for this antiquarian approach. Certainly no one would mistake this book for one of the nineteenth century, nor was that ever the intention. But style will forever remain a matter of taste, and the cyclical evolution of taste frequently involves stylistically backward glances and borrowings.

SMITH 356

51. A CATALOGUE OF AN EXHIBITION OF WALTONIANA
¶ BOSTON, THE CLUB OF ODD VOLUMES, 1912 (130 COPIES)

An engaging little catalogue and an example of the more modest publications done for the Club of Odd Volumes. Small as the work is, it contains an extensive amount of complicated bibliographical material, deftly handled and well printed. Considering that an average of some 400 items were done annually at the Press, the general level of printing and design is impressive, especially when one remembers how small the Press always remained.

SMITH 377

52. ORDINARY AND CANON OF THE MASS
¶ NEW YORK, THE H. W. GRAY COMPANY FOR NOVELLO AND CO., LTD., 1913 (ISSUED IN SHEETS)

An ecclesiastical work, these sheets contain the Order for Holy Communion and the Holy Chant. They are rubricated throughout and are the Press's last use of Goodhue's Merrymount type, set here in double columns. The Holy Chant is as handsomely printed as the leaves of music accompanying *The Altar Book* of 1896. The Press did extensive work on music books for both the Oliver Ditson Company and Schirmer's of Boston and New York. As only title-pages and introductory matter were printed at the Press for Ditson, and just the covers for Schirmer's, these items were never listed in the Press bibliography.

SMITH 389

53. THE STORY OF GEORGE CROWNINSHIELD'S YACHT CLEOPATRA'S BARGE, BY FRANCIS B. CROWNINSHIELD
¶ BOSTON, PRIVATELY PRINTED, 1913

Specially designed endpapers by Dwiggins, printed in three colors, and an elegant gold-stamped red binding evoking the logbook of 1816 make this a sumptuous Merrymount edition. No doubt the Crowninshield pocket permitted—and insisted upon—a more than usual elegance. The book boasts numerous gravure illustrations and a well-printed text in Scotch-face. A stylish volume, this logbook should be compared with Cleopatra's Barge II— another yacht, another era, and another Merrymount production (no. 135).

SMITH 390

54. A LOVER'S MOODS, BY BERTRAM DOBELL
¶ CLEVELAND, OHIO, THE ROWFANT CLUB, 1914 (200 COPIES)

A Lover's Moods was printed for the Rowfant Club. The red border is initialed "C" for T. M. Cleland and the type is Caslon. The sonnet form of these poems, together with the length of the lines, creates a somewhat square page. As a result, the book is rather wider for its height than is typical of most Merrymount books.

SMITH 402

55. NAPOLEON, AN ESSAY BY WILLIAM MAKEPEACE THACKERAY, WITH REPRODUCTIONS OF FIVE ORIGINAL SKETCHES BY THE AUTHOR
¶ PRIVATELY PRINTED, 1915 (75 COPIES)

Seventy-five copies of this privately printed book with original sketches by the author were printed on a thin handmade paper with the Merrymount watermark. There is somewhat more "show-through" than usual in the printing, but it does not detract from the beauty of the book. The range of text paper used by the Press was extensive and highly varied. Many of these papers are either no longer available to or commercially viable for the average printer. However, at the time they contributed considerably to the richness of many a Merrymount volume.

SMITH 421

56. A CATALOGUE OF THE COLLECTION OF PRINTS FROM THE LIBER
STUDIORUM OF JOSEPH MALLORD TURNER FORMED BY THE LATE
FRANCIS BULLARD OF BOSTON, MASSACHUSETTS, AND
BEQUEATHED BY HIM TO THE MUSEUM OF FINE ARTS IN BOSTON
¶ BOSTON, PRIVATELY PRINTED, 1916 (300 COPIES)

Many illustrated books were produced over the years by the Press, sometimes with separate
portfolios of illustration. The Press utilized virtually every process, including etching, engraving, collotype, pochoir, woodblock, and photogravure. Of this volume Updike wrote:
"The reproduction of the prints was attended with difficulty, for the originals could not be
taken from the Museum and so trial proofs of each of our plates had to be brought there,
compared, and corrected. I have spoken of problems in printing which, if surmounted,
should be invisible. There was such a problem in this book. Many of the pictures were not
uniform in depth, so that if they were to occupy the same relative position from the top
margin of the book throughout, the distance between them and the first line of type, which
also had to be invariable in position, differed. We overcame this difficulty by never al-
lowing two pictures to face each other, so that in turning the page the eye did not catch the
discrepancy."

SMITH 437

57. THE BOOK OF THE HOMELESS (LE LIVRE DE SANS FOYER), EDITED
BY EDITH WHARTON
¶ NEW YORK, CHARLES SCRIBNER'S SONS, 1916 (175 LARGE-PAPER
COPIES)

The correspondence between Wharton, Updike, Scribner's, and other contributors to *The
Book of the Homeless* is enormous, and reflects the extensive time needed to produce this
difficult work, issued in both regular and special editions. This was a charitable undertaking, and Updike bore it without any outward sign of frustration. The regular edition, alas,
is not one of the Press's finest moments, but the deluxe large-paper copies—this one on Van
Gelder paper—are handsome. *The Book of the Homeless* is filled with reproductions of works
by Monet, Renoir, and Sargent, and the prose and poetry of James, Rostand, Conrad, and
Cocteau, among others—it even boasts a score by Stravinsky—all specially donated for the
ultimate benefit of Belgian World War I refugees.

SMITH 451

58. NEWARK, A SERIES OF ENGRAVINGS ON WOOD BY RUDOLPH
RUZICKA, WITH AN APPRECIATION,
BY WALTER PRITCHARD EATON
¶ NEWARK, NEW JERSEY, THE CARTERET BOOK CLUB, 1917
(200 COPIES)

The Merrymount Press had a particularly happy association with the artist-designer
Rudolph Ruzicka. Certainly artists like Cleland, Dwiggins, and Sidney Lawton Smith

served the Press well, but Ruzicka's wood engravings had a special, clear, spare quality that seemed to share the Press's aesthetic. Much of Ruzicka's work was used over the years, including the now famous New Year's cards, issued by The Merrymount Press from 1912 until 1942. In this volume the engravings–highly regarded by critics–are the chief feature of the book.

SMITH 460

59. PIERROT'S VERSES, BY MARIA DE ACOSTA SARGENT
¶ PRIVATELY PRINTED, 1917

Maria Sargent's delightful little volume, with its sprightly chinoiserie figure printed in red on the title-page, is one of the Press's gems. Ever since Updike and then Cleland introduced them, these orientalized, French eighteenth-century design conceits became a stock-in-trade for the Press, appearing in the most unexpected places, including an advertisement for a local laundry! The binding paper on the *Pierrot* is a stylized pattern of plant leaves, and the type used is Oxford.

SMITH 473

60. MEMOIRS OF THE PRIVATE LIFE OF MARIE ANTOINETTE, BY
JEANNE LOUISE HENRIETTE CAMPAN, WITH A MEMOIR OF
MADAME CAMPAN BY F. BARRIÈRE
¶ NEW YORK, BRENTANO'S, 1917 [2 VOLS.]

Updike was very pleased with the Press's two-volume edition of Madame Campan's *Memoirs*, intended as a companion set to the Cellini *Life*, also printed for Brentano's. Updike speaks on the inspiration for title-page and binding: "The title-page is a reproduction of an old engraved title-page; and the cover reproduces a binding said to have been executed by Derôme for Marie Antoinette . . . its design covering uninterrupted the whole back, the old-fashioned 'ribs' being done away with. The bindings of many books printed at the Press have been arranged here. Some of them are simple affairs with cloth backs and marbled cloth or paper sides; others adaptions of old designs which, while not always remarkable, have the advantage of being 'on good terms' with the printing inside the cover–which is saying a good deal."

SMITH 475

61. JAMES BROWNE
¶ BOSTON, PRINTED BY D. B. UPDIKE AT THE MERRYMOUNT
PRESS, 1917

Inevitably, much allusive period printing was done, for so much of the material printed by the Press concerned seventeenth- and eighteenth-century New England Americana. Updike felt this was one of the Press's most successful period productions. Even in so slim a volume as this, there is considerable variety of type arrangement, borders, and decorations. This care extends even to the decorative paper of the binding, which reproduces what appears to be a floral cotton chintz of the period.

SMITH 476

62. PORTRAITS OF WHISTLER: A CRITICAL STUDY AND ICONOGRAPHY, BY A. E. GALLATIN, WITH FORTY ILLUSTRATIONS
¶ NEW YORK, JOHN LANE COMPANY, LONDON, JOHN LANE, THE BODLEY HEAD, 1918 (250 COPIES)

The Portraits of Whistler was one of several books on the artist done by The Merrymount Press. Elegant and satisfactory in every way from the cover to the clear and eminently readable catalogue entries, this volume gives pleasure to the beholder. As an example of the art catalogue genre of its day, it was, and indeed still is, exemplary.

SMITH 492

63. BIBLIOTHECA AMERICANA, CATALOGUE OF THE JOHN CARTER BROWN LIBRARY IN BROWN UNIVERSITY, PROVIDENCE, RHODE ISLAND, VOLUME I [PARTS I, II]
¶ PROVIDENCE, PUBLISHED BY THE LIBRARY, 1919 (REGULAR EDITION 250 COPIES; 25 COPIES WERE PRINTED ON HANDMADE PAPER)

Perhaps one of the best designed book catalogues printed in America—unfortunately in a severely limited edition—the *Bibliotheca Americana* is one of the finest achievements of The Merrymount Press. Catalogues test the mettle of most designers and printers, and this one was particularly onerous. Updike indicated that "typographic requirements of this work in diacritical marks, symbols, superior letters, and the like, and the careful proof-reading needful for entries in Latin, Italian, German, Dutch, and other languages make the production one requiring constant care." This *Catalogue*, published in the first year after the World War, signaled the beginning of the Press's finest period, culminating in 1930 with its masterwork, *The Book of Common Prayer*.

SMITH 509

64. THE ISLE OF PINES, 1688, AN ESSAY IN BIBLIOGRAPHY BY WORTHINGTON CHAUNCEY FORD
¶ BOSTON, THE CLUB OF ODD VOLUMES, 1920 (151 COPIES)

Gold-lettered black cloth spine, marbled paper cover over boards, handmade paper for text, and superlative printing make *The Isle of Pines* a far from standard production. While the book is conservative, it manages to be elegant without being old-fashioned. It is frequently those designs which strive to be "modern" that date most readily.

SMITH 523

65. JULIAN ALDEN WEIR, AN APPRECIATION OF HIS LIFE AND WORKS, WITH ILLUSTRATIONS
¶ NEW YORK, THE CENTURY CLUB, 1921 (718 COPIES)

The Merrymount Press, when dealing with contemporary subjects, often attempted, as in this volume on the artist Julian Alden Weir, to create a more modern look. Indeed, the binding and overall design here seem inventive and fresh.

SMITH 539

66. NOTES AND JOURNAL OF TRAVEL IN EUROPE, 1804–1805, BY WASHINGTON IRVING, ILLUSTRATIONS IN AQUATINT BY RUDOLPH RUZICKA, IN THREE VOLUMES
¶ NEW YORK, THE GROLIER CLUB, 1921, (257 COPIES)

Irving's three-volume *Journal* for The Grolier Club has been one of the Press's most admired productions. The attractiveness of Ruzicka's aquatints, heightened with water colors, lends a special grace to the book. The great care with which the volume was produced accounts for the high price it initially (and subsequently) commanded in the book market.

SMITH 542

67. PRINTING TYPES, THEIR HISTORY, FORMS, AND USE, A STUDY IN SURVIVALS, BY DANIEL BERKELEY UPDIKE, WITH ILLUSTRATIONS [2 VOLS.]
¶ CAMBRIDGE, HARVARD UNIVERSITY PRESS, LONDON, HUMPHREY MILFORD, OXFORD UNIVERSITY PRESS, 1922

Perhaps no other work on a similar topic has had so far-reaching an impact on typographical scholarship as the two-volume *Printing Types*. The lectures on printing which Updike gave at Harvard, representing years of study and investigation, formed the basis of this important work. He had always demonstrated his knowledge of types and style in the books printed by the Press, but it was this typographical exegesis that showed his learning, winning him the honor of being called the "Scholar-Printer." It went through several editions during his lifetime, and is still in print today. It is sometimes referred to as the "Printer's Bible."

SMITH 548

68. THE FELICITIES OF SIXTY, BY ISAAC H. LIONBERGER
¶ BOSTON, THE CLUB OF ODD VOLUMES, 1922 (101 COPIES)

Updike shares with Bruce Rogers a sure sense of the appropriate and interesting in typographical ornament. *The Felicities of Sixty* is the earliest volume set entirely in Janson type by the Press. Updike esteemed Janson but could not procure sufficient type for larger works until later in the decade.

SMITH 550

69. DIBDIN'S GHOST, & BOCCACCIO, BY EUGENE FIELD
   ¶ 1922 (500 COPIES)

The Merrymount Press was very fortunate in securing the patronage of William K. Bixby, a St. Louis bibliophile. It was Mr. Bixby's habit to commission books and facsimiles based on items from his own collection. This volume–and the two following–show the creativity elicited from Updike on Bixby's behalf. These works often have a breezier style than those equally lush commissions prepared for his New England clients.

SMITH 553

70. TWO POEMS BY EUGENE FIELD REPRODUCED FROM
   THE ORIGINAL MSS
   ¶ PRIVATELY PRINTED FOR W. K. BIXBY [1922] (250 COPIES)

The early 1920s, coming in the aftermath of the First World War, was a period of affirmation, exultation, and extravagance. No doubt Mr. Bixby insisted on, and paid for, the very best of everything when it came to his books. Great care and ingenuity were required for all the Bixby works. Produced over a concentrated period of time, they were nevertheless inventive and appropriately divergent in their designs. This volume could not be more different than the preceding entry nor the following, although all were designed at roughly the same time.

SMITH 554

71. TWO LETTERS, GENERAL ANTHONY WAYNE TO GENERAL
   SCHUYLER, LETTER FROM GEORGE WASHINGTON TO THE JUDGE
   ADVOCATE GENERAL
   ¶ PRIVATELY PRINTED FOR W. K. BIXBY, 1922 (250 COPIES)

The title-page reads that this volume was printed for "Historical Societies and Personal Friends." Bixby apparently gave away most of the copies printed. Indeed, it is difficult to find a copy of one of his books printed by the Press that does *not* have a presentation in his hand.

These letters are executed in faithful facsimile, and the delightful cover is taken from a *toile* devoted to an American theme. The book's shape and size conform to the paper size of the facsimile letter within.

SMITH 555

72. A CHOICE OF MANUSCRIPTS AND BOOKBINDINGS FROM THE
   LIBRARY OF ISABELLA STEWART GARDNER, FENWAY COURT
   ¶ 1922

This is the second catalogue done for the library of Isabella Stewart Gardner. The first bibliography of 1906 was so riddled with errors (errors which Mrs. Gardner refused to acknowledge) that Updike left off the Press's imprint in retaliation. A number of copies of that edition contain corrections made, after the fact, in Mrs. Gardner's own hand. This volume, however, is bibliographically and linguistically sound, and in the same style as the 1906 edition. Clearly Mrs. Gardner had learned her lesson. Indeed, the Press subsequently printed a series of guides to her collection, and a major catalogue of her paintings as well.

SMITH 560

73. BENJAMIN FRANKLIN ON BALLOONS, A LETTER WRITTEN FROM PASSY, FRANCE
¶ SAINT LOUIS, PRIVATELY PRINTED FOR W. K. BIXBY, 1922 (250 COPIES)

In many ways the most charming of The Merrymount Press books printed for Bixby. Updike writes: "I had chosen for the title-page a reproduction of an old engraving of Franklin's house at Passy, with a Montgolfier balloon riding the sky, and as luck would have it I received at just the right moment a visit from the representative of the French paper-makers Canson and Montgolfier. Finding that the Montgolfier of this firm was a descendant of the famous aeronaut, I procured from him the paper for the booklet, water-marked with a balloon–for the Montgolfier balloon was made of paper from the same mill. For the cover paper an amusing 'balloon' design used by Oberkampff for a printed chintz was chosen, being redrawn for our purpose by Mr. Dwiggins. A quotation on the title-page from Franklin's prophetic letter about the future of air-warfare is not the least interesting feature of the book." Equally interesting to the observer should be the care brought to the design of so small an edition. Again, here is a case where money is no object, but a case where taste and sensibility are.

SMITH 563

74. THE WEDDING JOURNEY OF CHARLES AND MARTHA BABCOCK AMORY [2 VOLS.]
¶ BOSTON, PRIVATELY PRINTED, 1922 (100 COPIES)

Many of the books printed at The Merrymount Press required a great deal more work than just printing. This volume, for instance, had to be set up from the actual journal written by the author from 1833 to 1834. Not only was Mrs. Amory's handwriting extremely difficult to decipher, but the route itself, through obscure towns and villages, had to be verified by road maps of the period. Similarly, the Press verified the titles of art works from contemporary guide books. This work proved to be a painstaking and drawn-out process. Updike himself wrote both the preface and a résumé of chapter contents. It was, he wrote in a rare moment of self-congratulation, "a triumph of patience and ingenuity." The cover design reproduced that of the journal itself. The book was printed in two volumes, in an edition of 100 for private distribution. The type was Mountjoye. Clearly, The Merrymount Press did not insist upon type-ready manuscripts, but offered every service in the production of its works.

SMITH 567

75. THE JOURNAL OF MRS. JOHN AMORY, EDITED AND ARRANGED BY MARTHA C. CODMAN
¶ BOSTON, PRIVATELY PRINTED, 1923 (100 COPIES)

Another journal by a member of the Amory family. This volume, like the preceding one, has a subtle sumptuousness. The subtlety stems in part from Updike's own abhorrence of show, the sumptuousness from the fact that no expense was spared on the part of the client. These books, though cited in the literature on the Press, are rarely seen, having been printed in small editions that were never commercially available at the time of their issue.

SMITH 572

76. STEPHEN CRANE, BY THOMAS L. RAYMOND
¶ NEWARK, NEW JERSEY, THE CARTERET BOOK CLUB, 1923 (250 COPIES)

A frequently cited work for the Carteret Book Club, this volume has a penetrating portrait of Crane by Rudolph Ruzicka printed in black. A paste-paper cover–in rich blue with a crimson cloth spine and decorated gold-embossed leather label–encases a well-printed text in Oxford type on handmade wove paper. It is one of Merrymount's little jewels.

SMITH 575

77. A JOURNEY TO INDIA, 1921–1922, CASUAL COMMENT BY ALBERT FARWELL BEMIS
¶ BOSTON, PRIVATELY PRINTED, 1923

Although printed soon after *Stephen Crane*, and also set in Oxford type, Bemis's essay on his Indian journey differs much in character. The book is illustrated with the author's own photographs, and the altered proportions, spacing, and warm-toned paper create a design flavor quite distinct from that of the Crane.

SMITH 578

78. CHINESE PAINTING OF LI LUNG-MEIN, 1070–1106, BY AGNES E. MEYER
¶ NEW YORK, DUFFIELD & COMPANY, 1923 (DELUXE EDITION OF 300 COPIES PRINTED ON JAPANESE PAPER ACCOMPANIED BY A PORTFOLIO OF 20 REPRODUCTIONS)

The deluxe edition of *Chinese Painting*, with its separate portfolio of reproductions, won the A.I.G.A. medal for the most distinguished example of bookmaking in 1923. The edition is printed on handmade Japanese paper with decorative Japanese endleaf and cover papers. It contains, in addition to the contents of the trade edition, a catalogue of the artist's paintings indexed according to the Chinese titles. The extensive use of Chinese characters within a text of Mountjoye and Oxford Roman types led to what Updike amusingly considered an unwarranted reputation for scholarly printing. He maintained that each character had to be labelled "This side up" before being placed in the text. Despite the Press's lack of a thorough knowledge of the Chinese language, the work–falling about mid-point in the life of The Merrymount Press–was one of its most successful productions, and justified the somewhat amazing price in 1923 of $100.

SMITH 590

79. IN THE DAY'S WORK, BY DANIEL BERKELEY UPDIKE, LIMITED EDITION
¶ CAMBRIDGE, HARVARD UNIVERSITY PRESS, 1924 (260 COPIES)

The limited edition of a selection of Updike's essays is printed in Caslon type. It contains eleven examples of the Press's typography, some in color, and what is unquestionably one of Updike's most playful colophons. Winship wrote that the works illustrated "came nearest to satisfying him [Updike] . . . with a colophon as individualistic as anything he ever allowed himself."* An admirable production bound in rich marbled cloth.

*George Parker Winship, *Daniel Berkeley Updike and the Merrymount Press of Boston Massachusetts, 1860, 1894, 1941* (Rochester, New York: The Printing House of Leo Hart, 1947), 114.

SMITH 605

80. A DISSERTATION UPON ENGLISH TYPOGRAPHICAL FOUNDERS AND FOUNDERIES, BY EDWARD ROWE MORES, EDITED BY D. B. UPDIKE
¶ NEW YORK, THE GROLIER CLUB, 1924 (250 COPIES)

The third book printed for The Grolier Club, here on Vidalon paper, with portraits, genealogical fold-out table, and facsimiles. Mores's idiosyncratic treatise contains an introduction by Updike, who wrote: "The decorations, made up from varying combinations of two or three typographical flowers, are worth looking at." Updike also added that it was "the most careful literary performance I have ever attempted."

SMITH 607

81. GASTON LACHAISE, SIXTEEN REPRODUCTIONS IN COLLOTYPE OF THE SCULPTOR'S WORK, EDITED BY A. E. GALLATIN
¶ NEW YORK, E. P. DUTTON & COMPANY, 1924 (400 COPIES)

Sixteen full-page illustrations in collotype are here accompanied by a short introduction by A. E. Gallatin. This attractive if somewhat restrained "art book" is the kind of volume that satisfied the collector in the early 1920s. Made for a limited audience, the book contains a catalogue raisonné of Lachaise's work.

SMITH 608

82. A NOTE ON THE DISCOVERY OF A NEW PAGE OF POETRY IN WILLIAM BLAKE'S MILTON, BY S. FOSTER DAMON, ILLUSTRATED BY FACSIMILE REPRODUCTIONS
¶ PRINTED FOR THE CLUB OF ODD VOLUMES, THE MERRYMOUNT PRESS, 1925 (150 COPIES)

The Blake book is noteworthy as much for being an expression of publishing interest of the time as an example of fine printing. Barely fourteen pages in length with three full-color illustrations, all attractively bound in marbled paper over boards, this quarto volume epitomizes the willingness (and the money available) to indulge in handsome and expensive bibliographical exercise. Much of this kind of printing would come to an end with the Depression.

SMITH 615

83. AN ACCOUNT OF THE DEDICATION OF THE WEST WINDOW OF
ST. JOHN'S CHURCH, BEVERLY FARMS
¶ PRIVATELY PRINTED, 1925 (130 COPIES)

Even more characteristic of printing and binding indulgence of the period is this gilt morocco-bound quarto on the dedication of a stained-glass window in Beverly Farms, Massachusetts. Printed in Poliphilus on fine handmade paper rubricated throughout, including a full-page gravure illustration, this was an enormously expensive memento – an almost regal conceit. It is an example of superb printing and period binding.

SMITH 620

84. THE PUBLIC LATIN SCHOOL OF BOSTON IN THE WORLD WAR,
1914–1918, A ROLL OF HONOR
¶ BOSTON, 1925 (26 COPIES)

One of the most sober and beautiful books in the history of The Merrymount Press, this volume, because of its nature and severely limited edition, is largely unknown to the bibliophile. It seems best to let Updike himself speak about the work: "The book at first sight seems easy to print, but the proviso that it was to be kept in a glass case and a page turned every day involved the presentation of entries which must be complete on each two facing pages. The pages dedicated to men who died in war were rubricated and each inscription had a page to itself; but for men still living the inscription had – in printer's language – to be 'run in.' Further stipulations were 1) that the names should be arranged in strictly alphabetical order, and 2) that there could be no omission in each record. To see how these difficulties were overcome and the rules complied with, one must see the book. It was set entirely in Poliphilus and Blado type. The pages were surrounded by emblematic borders, in which the arms of the United States, eagles bearing olive branches, and heads of Liberty figure in white on black background – one of the earliest 'native' American type ornaments, produced just after the War of 1812. I have had quite enough of books 'with borders on every page,' but bordered pages were adopted here since no more than two pages were to be shown at once."

SMITH 625

85. THE GHOST IN THE ATTIC AND OTHER VERSES, BY
GEORGE S. BRYAN
¶ NEW YORK, ALFRED A. KNOPF, 1926

An example of commercial printing for the publisher Alfred Knopf in the mid-twenties. The book has a typographical wrapper, decorative paper boards, and a well-composed text and title-page. The Press printed books for over four dozen major publishing houses including Macmillan, Simon and Schuster, and Random House. By the 1920s, Merrymount's reputation was worldwide, and the Press was approached by an ever-widening circle of clients.

SMITH 633

86. FROM SHEEP PASTURE TO FLOWER GARDEN, A PAPER READ AT THE CASTINE GARDEN CLUB BY A MEMBER
¶ BOSTON, PRIVATELY PRINTED, 1926

Printed for a member of a Maine garden club, this small (ten-page) booklet shows the same care as that given to larger, more extensive editions done by the Press. The type, decorations, composition, and printing received the same meticulous attention accorded every Merrymount production. This booklet exemplifies the fact that minor works were as seriously designed and executed at the Press as those deemed major.

SMITH 639

87. THE HIGHER CITIZENSHIP, TWO ADDRESSES, BY ALFRED L. BAKER
¶ CHICAGO, PRIVATELY PRINTED, 1927 (750 COPIES)

The first full use by the Press of Van Krimpen's Lutetia type. This elegant, small, privately issued book was printed on machine and handmade paper; both editions are bound becomingly in either marbled or decorated papers. Updike's sensitivity to type and his excitement in using newly acquired faces are conveyed in this work.

SMITH 653

88. THE COMPLETE ANGLER, BY ISAAC WALTON, INTRODUCTION BY BLISS PERRY AND DECORATIONS BY W. A. DWIGGINS
¶ BOSTON, C. E. GOODSPEED & CO., 1928 (600 COPIES)

Binding and decoration by W. A. Dwiggins. This eminently readable and pleasurable *Angler* compares well with Bruce Rogers's treatment of the same text. Both are small in scale and depend on a judicious balance of decoration with type arrangement, and both are successful in their separate ways.

SMITH 666

89. A CHRONOLOGICAL LIST OF THE BOOKS PRINTED AT THE KELMSCOTT PRESS, NOW IN THE LIBRARY OF MARSDEN J. PERRY OF PROVIDENCE, RHODE ISLAND
¶ [1927] (800 COPIES)

This *List* was printed for members of The Grolier Club. The composition, decorations, and choice of British handmade paper betoken a gentle and respectful nod to William Morris. There is a wedding of useful text coupled with a subtle use of historically allusive design which creates balance between the past and the present.

SMITH 669

90. EGYPTIAN LITERATURE, A LECTURE BY ARTHUR CRUTTENDEN MACE, LATE ASSOCIATE CURATOR, DEPARTMENT OF EGYPTIAN ART
¶ NEW YORK, THE METROPOLITAN MUSEUM OF ART, 1928 (250 COPIES)

Printed on handmade paper for the Metropolitan Museum. This book, with its cloud like binding, decorations, and superb craftsmanship, is typical of the Press's quality and design, yet represents a far from typical standard of excellence for American printing. The Merrymount Press was certainly not the only fine printer of books during the first half of the twentieth century, yet its work compared favorably with the very best of the time.

SMITH 670

91. WEST RUNNING BROOK, BY ROBERT FROST
¶ NEW YORK, HENRY HOLT AND COMPANY, 1928 (1,000 COPIES)

West Running Brook was designed solely by John Bianchi. As good-looking and successful as the work is, it has a different feeling from the usual Updike/Bianchi product. The design seems more open, with more leading between lines and perhaps larger margins than customary. Even the design of maple leaves on the cover, appropriate to the subject, makes this volume distinctive. *West Running Brook* suggests that the two partners had divergent approaches to designing, which became apparent when they worked on their own. This was particularly true of Bianchi, who as the younger partner might have felt more attuned to the modern. Many of the books after Updike's death have a considerably different character.

SMITH 673

92. HUNT CLUBS AND COUNTRY CLUBS IN AMERICA
¶ BOSTON, PRIVATELY PRINTED, 1928

Employing Oxford type with a single handsome and apposite canine cut on the title-page, this book is both solid and forthright. The diversity of subjects treated at The Merrymount Press is obvious from looking at the focus of its first dozen books printed during 1928: music, poetry, fishing, memorial tablets, religion, British fine printing, Egyptian literature, American silver, law schools, and as in the case here, hunt and country clubs. What is admirable about the Press's treatment of these disparate topics is the care taken in rendering designs appropriate to the subject—to wit: the delightful running dog-cut on the title-page, and the hunting-pink cloth cover of this book.

SMITH 674

93. THE FORM OF CONSECRATION OF ST. GEORGE'S CHAPEL
¶ MIDDLETOWN, RHODE ISLAND, ST. GEORGE'S SCHOOL, 1928
(600 COPIES)

For sixty-five years, this small book, printed on the occasion of a private school's chapel dedication, has been one of the more admired and sought after Merrymount Press books. The year 1928 was a highly charged one for the Press, concerned as it was with ideas for printing *The Book of Common Prayer*. There are affinities here with both the trial pages for the latter work and for the prayer book itself. Set in Janson, rubricated, decorated only with Caslon fleurons (as was also true with the finished prayer book), this work is charged with considerable power. Perfectly printed and bound, it is a miniature masterpiece.

SMITH 679

94. QUARTO CLUB PAPERS
¶ NEW YORK, PRINTED FOR THE MEMBERS, 1929 (99 COPIES)

The Quarto Club, founded in 1926, had sixteen members, of whom Elmer Adler, Jerome Kern, and Bruce Rogers were among the most significant. The delightful cuts and decorative letters are printed here in "burnt ochre," matching the damask endpapers which frame this luxuriously printed series of papers. The production must have pleased those most discriminating bibliophiles.

SMITH 682

95. OLD MRS. CHUNDLE, A SHORT STORY BY THOMAS HARDY
¶ NEW YORK, CROSBY GAIGE, 1929 (755 COPIES)

Hardy's short story is effectively treated in this volume printed for Crosby Gaige: Janson type on Sanders handmade paper bound in decorated paper. The volume was distributed by Random House. The economics of bookmaking during the latter half of the twentieth century precluded commercial companies, except, most notably, James Laughlin's New Directions, from indulging in such productions as this, and it fell to private presses to issue limited editions of modern authors. As part of this run, Hardy's story was also printed in thirteen copies on gray French Ingres paper.

SMITH 683

96. THE FIRST AMERICAN BIBLE, A LEAF FROM A COPY OF THE BIBLE
TRANSLATED INTO THE INDIAN LANGUAGE BY JOHN ELIOT AND
PRINTED AT CAMBRIDGE, 1662, WITH AN ACCOUNT BY GEORGE
PARKER WINSHIP
¶ BOSTON, CHARLES E. GOODSPEED AND COMPANY, 1929
(157 COPIES)

When Goodspeed's acquired an incomplete Eliot Indian Bible, they turned to George Parker Winship for an essay to enable them to issue a leaf book. The combination of a leaf from an icon of early American printing and the allusive early twentieth-century design make this an interesting document. It is the only leaf book printed by the Press.

SMITH 685

97. LETTERS FROM AN OLD SPORTSMAN TO A YOUNG ONE, BY
A. HENRY HIGGINSON
¶ GARDEN CITY, NEW YORK, DOUBLEDAY, DORAN AND COMPANY,
INC., 1929 (1,500 COPIES)

Higginson's book, geared to a larger commercial publishing house, seems to slip into another design key. It *looks* like a commercial book of its day, and it looks and feels different from other Merrymount work. Which is to say, by way of compliment, that it suits its need and adapts to its use, and by so doing, it changes stylistically. A limited edition of 201 copies was also printed for Doubleday on Aurelian paper.

SMITH 686

98. PUNCH AND JUDY, ILLUSTRATED BY GEORGE CRUIKSHANK,
FOREWORD BY TONY SARG
¶ NEW YORK, RIMINGTON & HOOPER, 1929 (376 COPIES)

Punch and Judy (actually distributed by Doubleday, Doran) was one of "The Savoy Editions." Individually boxed with an interesting cover-paper-board binding, this appealing work, with many delightful Cruikshank illustrations, made an enticing product for the book-buying public—unknowingly on the cusp of the Great Depression.

SMITH 688

99. AN EARLY AMERICAN QUEEN ANNE ESCRITOIRE, 1715–1730
¶ PRIVATELY PRINTED [1929] (200 COPIES)

An earlier Merrymount Press book (no. 102), once described as "austere and solemn without being plain," was compared to a piece of American Colonial furniture. Here, Ross Maynard, the owner of this early American desk, remarks that his piece of furniture had charm and individuality as well as delicacy and decorative quality. We might indeed say the same of the book itself and its restrained binding of gold-stamped Fabriano paper, gilt top-edge, marbled endpapers, and simple, stately title-page, all superbly printed on handmade paper.

SMITH 694

100. THE GLORY OF THE NIGHTINGALES, BY EDWARD ARLINGTON
ROBINSON
¶ NEW YORK, THE MACMILLAN COMPANY, 1930 (500 COPIES)

Robinson's signed, limited edition book of poetry is sober and handsome. The dark blue binding is impressed in blind, the dark blue spine label is stamped in gold, and the only decoration is a fleuron on the rubricated title-page. The Janson type is particularly well printed on a very beautiful, crisp white paper. This volume evidently proved successful and the Press printed a second Robinson book for Macmillan the following year in a similar format.

SMITH 709

101. THE FABLES OF JEAN DE LA FONTAINE, NEWLY TRANSLATED BY JOSEPH AUSLANDER AND JACQUES LE CLERCQ, DECORATIONS BY RUDOLPH RUZICKA [2 VOLS.]
¶ NEW YORK, THE LIMITED EDITIONS CLUB, 1930 (1,500 COPIES)

This two-volume work is decorated with Ruzicka illustrations throughout and printed in Janson type. At the time, Updike was using Janson extensively, and unconscious intimations of the forthcoming *Book of Common Prayer* are evident, if faintly, on the title-page. Yet the book possesses its own individuality and character, indeed, as the subject warranted.

SMITH 711

102. THE BOOK OF COMMON PRAYER OF THE PROTESTANT EPISCOPAL CHURCH IN THE UNITED STATES OF AMERICA, TOGETHER WITH THE PSALTER
¶ PRINTED FOR THE COMMISSION, 1928 (500 COPIES ON PAPER, 5 ON VELLUM)

One of the most famous and beautiful books ever printed in America is the Episcopal Church's *Book of Common Prayer* of 1928. Its history reached back to the prayer book of 1892–93, and its genesis was prolonged and difficult. It was a prize not easily won, and less easily produced. The intense competition to print this work for J. P. Morgan, Jr. aside, its preparation was the result of the most painstaking attention of heart and mind on the part of Updike, Bianchi, and the Press. For Updike it was the culmination of everything he believed in and knew; and every facet of his personality and sensibility were called upon to produce this masterpiece of print and spirit. The specially procured Janson type here assumes a rare majesty. The sober elegance of page after page of superbly printed text, both distinct and eminently readable, makes this a work at once fresh and everlasting.

SMITH 713

103. WAR BOOKS, BY H. M. TOMLINSON
¶ CLEVELAND, THE ROWFANT CLUB, 1930 (215 COPIES)

The Book of Common Prayer behind him, Updike was now free to wrest himself from that particular vision, though still experimenting with his much loved Janson type. This small book is much admired. Great care was taken in the choice of the distinctive decorated paper that covers the binding and box, suggesting armaments exploding in the night.

SMITH 714

104. MERLIN, BY CLIVE FURST
¶ NEW YORK, 1930 (300 COPIES)

Printed on Fabriano and Zanders paper, Clive Furst's poem on Merlin is masterful and spare. The Janson type looks particularly good in this wide-margined setting. Some copies are bound in the same dark gray-brown Fabriano paper for cover, endleaves, and half-title page, which gives a feeling of mystery as one opens the book.

SMITH 722

105. THE COLONIAL PRINTER, BY LAWRENCE C. WROTH
¶ NEW YORK, THE GROLIER CLUB, 1931 (300 COPIES)

The author of this book, Lawrence Wroth, was librarian of the John Carter Brown Library. The price of the volume in the Depression year 1931 was $27.50, a considerable sum at the time. Remarking on it three years later, Updike wrote: "This very straightforward piece of work was executed in Mountjoye type, our intention being to make its typography wholly subservient to Mr. Wroth's text. Like most Grolier Club publishing, this book was issued in a limited edition at a fairly high price, though it is a pity that a work so valuable to students is restricted to a class of readers who seldom have occasion to make practical use of it." It has since been frequently reprinted elsewhere.

SMITH 729

106. SIDNEY LAWTON SMITH, DESIGNER, ETCHER, ENGRAVER
¶ BOSTON, CHARLES E. GOODSPEED & CO., 1931 (200 COPIES)

Depression or not, limited editions continued to be printed, although the momentum slackened somewhat. There was still money enough for some individuals to continue indulging their taste in fine books. Sidney Lawton Smith, who had provided etchings and illustrations for the Press earlier in the century, was well-known for his bookplates. This volume includes a checklist of them.

SMITH 730

107. PIUS XI ON CHRISTIAN MARRIAGE IN THE ORIGINAL LATIN WITH ENGLISH TRANSLATIONS
¶ NEW YORK, THE BARRY VAIL CORPORATION, 1931 (1,000 COPIES)

This sumptuous book was produced for John Barry Ryan in a considerable limited edition of 1,000, with a regular companion run of 25,000. The book would have been an extremely expensive undertaking at any time, and proved to be a problem on two counts. Updike wrote only about the typographical problems, but it was many years before the Press closed its accounts with Ryan, whose severe overspending during the Depression had overwhelmed him.

As for the physical book itself—with the Latin text on the left-hand page and the English translation on the right—there was the problem of keeping the two sides parallel. Since Latin is far more concise than English, Updike comments that "It was solved by beginning a new page at each section . . . and by setting the English translation in italic—a more condensed letter than roman—and leading it less than the Latin page. The volume [printed in Bodoni] is a very Italian affair and was purposely made as Roman as the Prayer Book is Anglican in effect."

SMITH 733

108. A CATALOGUE OF THE ALTSCHUL COLLECTION OF GEORGE MEREDITH IN THE YALE UNIVERSITY LIBRARY, COMPILED BY BERTHA COOLIDGE, INTRODUCTION BY CHAUNCEY BREWSTER TINKER
¶ PRIVATELY PRINTED, 1931 (500 COPIES)

This volume is a good example of the superbly designed catalogues printed by The Merrymount Press. Clearly laid out, well printed and bound, it is everything a catalogue should be. Today, such work—with handmade paper, letterpress printing, and gilt top-edge—would be a hugely costly endeavor, and would probably never be printed in such a manner.

SMITH 742

109. THE WALPOLE SOCIETY, IN PRAISE OF ANTIQUARIES, BY NORMAN M. ISHAM
¶ PRINTED BY THE SOCIETY, 1931 (110 COPIES)

Norman Isham's address given at the University Club in New York in February 1931 is elegantly printed for the Walpole Society. Its binding, a simple design derived from Roger Payne, complements the book perfectly. The bindings on Merrymount Press books were quite varied, always appropriate, and frequently beautiful.

SMITH 746

110. THE JAUNTS AND JOLLITIES OF MR. JOHN JORROCKS, BY R. S. SURTEES, INTRODUCTION BY A. EDWARD NEWTON
¶ NEW YORK, THE LIMITED EDITIONS CLUB, 1932 (1,500 COPIES)

It was no easy matter for the Limited Editions Club to continue publishing during the thirties, and yet the enterprise persevered. In 1932, The Merrymount Press opened its bibliographic year with their *Jaunts and Jollities*. The Introduction is by Newton and the sprightly illustrations by Gordon Ross.

SMITH 748

111. PEMBROKE COLLEGE IN BROWN UNIVERSITY, EXERCISES COMMEMORATIVE OF LIDA SHAW KING
¶ PROVIDENCE, RHODE ISLAND, PEMBROKE COLLEGE, 1932 (500 COPIES)

One of the earliest Merrymount Press books bound in paper designed and executed by Rosamond Loring, it is printed in Lutetia type on a lightly tinted wove paper. The type, the paper, the printing, and the binding all make this slight memorial text particularly appealing.

SMITH 749

112. THE ROCKEFELLER MCCORMICK TAPESTRIES, PHYLLIS ACKERMAN ¶ NEW YORK, OXFORD UNIVERSITY PRESS, LONDON [ETC.], [1932]

This volume, the largest ever produced at the Press—with loose plates, some in full color—would never have seen the light of day in 1932 had there not been some substantial under-writing of costs suggested by the names in the title. The size, however, was determined by the need for large reproductions for the early sixteenth-century tapestries. The text is printed in Janson and Caslon.

SMITH 752

113. THE BOOK OF THE OFFICIAL ACTS OF THE BISHOP OF MAINE ¶ 1933 (1 COPY PRINTED)

The last entry in the Smith Bibliography of 1934, *The Book of the Official Acts of the Bishop of Albany*, states that *Official Acts* for nine other Bishops, all in "one copy" were also pro-duced. Printed in Caslon and rubricated, the work is bibliographically "unique." But bibli-ographic uniqueness is sometimes a variable term: there would also have been overruns for filing although not for distribution, which only later might come to light, as indeed the copy in this exhibition proves.

SMITH 762

114. THE LIFE OF OUR LORD, BY CHARLES DICKENS, NOW FIRST PUBLISHED ¶ NEW YORK, SIMON AND SCHUSTER, 1934 (2,387 COPIES)

This first item in the supplementary Merrymount bibliography, like that of the very first entry of 1893, is pietistic. Printed in Caslon and Lettre Batarde, it is a conservative design befitting its subject. It was printed simultaneously in a limited edition along with the reg-ular first trade edition.

The making and marketing of books had changed considerably since the Press's incep-tion. By this time, the Press had been well-established for decades, and yet there is a stylis-tic affinity between the first book (no. 1) and this work which cannot be totally coincidental.

SMITH 763

115. CODEX QUARTUS SANCTI IACOBI (TURPIN'S CHRONICLE) ¶ [1934] (300 COPIES)

Printed almost entirely in Latin (with a prefatory note in French and a colophon in English), this solidly designed volume employs Monotype Caslon and recalls the setting of the Latin Tacitus of thirty years before. There the use of Merrymount type gave an antiquarian feeling almost completely absent from this volume. Interestingly, Updike employed various typefaces each time he printed Latin texts, but never in a "true" Roman letter unless one considers his use of Bodoni in the Papal encyclical (no. 107) as closest, at least, in spirit.

SMITH 765

116. SOME UNRECORDED LETTERS OF CAROLINE NORTON IN THE ALTSCHUL COLLECTION OF THE YALE UNIVERSITY LIBRARY, BY BERTHA COOLIDGE
¶ PRIVATELY PRINTED, 1934 (75 COPIES)

The letters of Caroline Norton, the granddaughter of Richard Brinsley Sheridan, accompanied the Frank Altschul bequest of the works of George Meredith to Yale in 1931 (no. 108). Some of these letters form the basis of this limited edition of seventy-five copies on handmade paper. The top edge is gilt and the binding is a red paste paper designed and executed by Rosamond Loring.

SMITH 766

117. ROBERT GROSSETESTE AND THE JEWS, BY LEE M. FRIEDMAN
¶ CAMBRIDGE, HARVARD UNIVERSITY PRESS, 1934

This interesting essay on Jews in thirteenth-century England contains illustrations in black and white and full color. The type is Monotype Caslon with a touch of black-letter. The opening paragraph initials are historiated, giving the book a slight period flavor. Updike no longer felt the need for anything more than a suggestion of period coloration in his books on early subjects. In this he was like many printers of his generation. The twenties and thirties saw the rise of the Bauhaus and Art Deco styles. The trend to "modernism" was in the air, and even independent designers did not wish to seem old-fashioned.

SMITH 767

118. THE PREFACE TO JOHNSON'S DICTIONARY OF THE ENGLISH LANGUAGE, 1755
¶ CLEVELAND, THE ROWFANT CLUB, 1934 (110 COPIES)

The Preface, from the first edition of Johnson's *Dictionary* housed at the Rowfant Library, was printed in a small edition for the members of the Club. Updike used Monotype Caslon with decorative period cuts bound in complementary marbled boards and cloth. So many books printed by The Merrymount Press were of an antiquarian nature that there was, by necessity, a more conservative stylistic tendency than if the texts had been of a consistently contemporary nature. However, period and contemporary approaches employed side by side tend to influence each other, and they did so at the Press.

SMITH 770

119. THOUGHTS ON THOMAS JEFFERSON, BY
HAROLD JEFFERSON COOLIDGE
¶ BOSTON, THE CLUB OF ODD VOLUMES, 1936

The Depression does not seem to have precluded the printing of small elegant books by members of The Club of Odd Volumes, as this delightful essay on Jefferson attests. Besides the colored gravure frontispiece after Rembrandt Peale, there are fold-out facsimile letters of Jefferson's printed on good paper and bound in paste-paper covers with gilt top-edge.

SMITH 809

120. TWO CENTURIES OF BRUCE ROGERS, WITH A PROLOGUE BY
CHRISTOPHER MORLEY
¶ NEW YORK, PHILIP C. DUSCHNES, 1937 (550 COPIES)

Duschnes's catalogue 25 is an interesting example of a mid-thirties bookseller's catalogue. Except those done for Goodspeed's, such works were not a commonplace item at Merrymount. Both Rogers and Updike were at the height of their respective careers at the time, and probably the two greatest figures in American printing during the first half of the twentieth century. Not uncharacteristically, they were wary of each other. These two men, so different in temperament, were understandably a little jealous of each other, sharing the narrow apex of their profession.

SMITH 815

121. THE OLD FARM, BY GERTRUDE WELD ARNOLD
¶ BOSTON, PRIVATELY PRINTED, 1937

Collotype illustration, Bewick cuts, and Monotype Caslon add to the considerable nostalgia of this privately printed work of the late 1930s. It was reminiscences of this sort which no doubt appealed to Updike, and he exercised his typical care in its composition and ornament. Stylized tree ornaments grace the spine titling.

SMITH 817

122. JESSIE THOMAS VINCENT
¶ BOSTON, 1937

Over the years, The Merrymount Press printed scores of memorial volumes, services, reminiscences, and the like. Some were but a single page, others full-length quartos. Somewhere between the two extremes were small books like this one for Jessie Vincent, typical in size and length.

SMITH 823

123. RICHARD SMITH, FIRST ENGLISH SETTLER OF THE
NARRAGANSETT COUNTRY, RHODE ISLAND, [WITH] NOTES BY
DANIEL BERKELEY UPDIKE
¶ BOSTON, THE MERRYMOUNT PRESS, 1937 (325 COPIES)

Updike's full-length study of his illustrious forebearer, Richard Smith, is one of some half-dozen books authored by Updike and printed by the Press. Although his anonymous hand seems to have been at work on many more by way of preface or printed notes, barely a dozen such items can be attributed to Updike at the Press.

SMITH 824

124. LANTERN SLIDES, BY MARY CADWALADER JONES
¶ PRIVATELY PRINTED, 1937

Mary Jones, who died in 1935, was Edith Wharton's sister-in-law, friend, and American business representative. Jones's daughter Beatrix (who became one of the country's premier women landscape architects) was married to Max Farrand, the first librarian of the Huntington Library. It was Farrand's Merrymount books which, when donated to the Huntington, became the nucleus of the largest collection of Merrymount material in the world. This book of family reminiscences was dedicated to the Farrands, both of whom wrote its prefatory note. All this sounded a somewhat elegiac note since Edith Wharton died the year *Lantern Slides* was published, ending an almost half-century's friendship with Updike, who himself was nearing the end of his life and career.

SMITH 825

125. THE WALL-PAINTINGS OF INDIA, CENTRAL ASIA & CEYLON, A
STUDY BY BENJAMIN ROWLAND, JR., WITH AN INTRODUCTION BY
ANANDA K. COOMARASWAMY
¶ BOSTON, PRINTED AT THE MERRYMOUNT PRESS, 1938 (500
COPIES WITH LOOSE REPRODUCTIONS IN PORTFOLIO)

This handsome portfolio revives Updike's use of Janson, which he had not used for some years. With an essay by Coomaraswamy and thirty plates in full color, the ensemble seems to signal an emergence from the depths of the Depression. The term "depression" has double significance as Updike himself, perhaps influenced by the vicissitudes of the time, had suffered a debilitating breakdown several years earlier. Having successfully overcome his illness, Updike, in some ways refreshed, spent his last years experimenting with old and new types and old and new effects.

SMITH 835

126. POEMS TO VERA, BY GEORGE STERLING
¶ NEW YORK, OXFORD UNIVERSITY PRESS, 1938

George Sterling's poems, following immediately after the Coomaraswamy portfolio, was printed for the Oxford University Press in Monotype Baskerville. Unlike the luxurious *Wall*

Paintings of India, these poems, at a price of $2.00, were expected to reach a larger audience. Despite its small size, it is a harmonious book, beautifully printed on good commercial paper with a well-composed title-page, good binding, and printed dust jacket.

SMITH 836

127. THE PICKWICK PAPERS, AN ADDRESS BEFORE THE CAXTON CLUB, BY J. CHRISTIAN BAY
¶ CHICAGO, THE CAXTON CLUB, 1938 (250 COPIES)

Christian Bay's address before the Caxton Club in January of 1938 and printed for the members of the Club, concerns, in part, the illustrations done for the first printing of Dickens's classic. One of Seymour's original illustrations is used again as the border for this work. There is, however, a lightness of touch which makes the book both contemporary and fresh.

SMITH 842

128. CARITA FIORENTINA
¶ PRIVATELY PRINTED, 1938 (200 COPIES)

Privately (and anonymously) printed, these appealing Florentine notes are well presented in this small Merrymount edition. The rubricated manuscript-style letters used on the title and in the opening initials throughout the text lend just the right touch to the Caslon typeface. Numerous small pamphlets like this one were printed at the Press from its inception, but they were listed as "Minor Printing" in Smith's bibliography. The choice of "minor" over "major" was often an arbitrary decision. Dozens of examples could be substituted for the *Carita*, each exhibiting the same design strength and variety.

SMITH 847

129. ADDRESS BY DANIEL BERKELEY UPDIKE AT THE OPENING OF THE UPDIKE COLLECTION OF BOOKS ON PRINTING
¶ PROVIDENCE PUBLIC LIBRARY, 1937 [1938] (175 COPIES)

No doubt this booklet was issued as a *post-facto* commemorative item containing Updike's remarks at the opening of the Updike Collection of printing at the Providence Public Library the previous year. This collection was later augmented with books primarily from Updike, and additional material from Julian Pearce Smith (The Merrymount Press bibliographer) and Edith Wetmore, Updike's kinswoman and herself a collector of books on fine printing.

SMITH 849

130. THE GROLIER CLUB, OFFICERS, COMMITTEES, CONSTITUTION AND BY-LAWS, MEMBERS, REPORTS OF OFFICERS AND COMMITTEES OF THE YEAR 1938
¶ NEW YORK, 1939

The Merrymount Press began printing The Grolier Club's *Yearbook* in 1939, introducing a format which, with slight variations, has continued to this day. Updike was elected an honorary member of the Club in 1926, and fourteen years later, when he was eighty years old, the Club honored him by mounting the largest commemorative exhibition ever held of the Press's work.

SMITH 856

131. AN ACCOUNT OF CALLIGRAPHY & PRINTING IN THE SIXTEENTH CENTURY, ATTRIBUTED TO CHRISTOPHER PLANTIN, TRANSLATION AND NOTES BY RAY NASH, AND FOREWORD BY STANLEY MORISON
¶ CAMBRIDGE, MASSACHUSETTS, DEPARTMENT OF PRINTING AND GRAPHIC ARTS, HARVARD COLLEGE LIBRARY, 1940 (250 COPIES)

This book on sixteenth-century calligraphy and printing has contributions by Ray Nash (who became a formidable scholar and teacher in the printing arts), and Stanley Morison (who initially came to visit Updike as a young "pilgrim"). Printed under the aegis of the recently formed Harvard College Library's Department of Printing and Graphic Arts, established by Philip Hofer, the book seems to symbolize and herald the impending end of the Updike era at The Merrymount Press.

SMITH 876

132. THE ELEMENTS OF LETTERING, BY JOHN HOWARD BENSON AND ARTHUR GRAHAM CAREY
¶ JOHN STEVENS, NEWPORT, RHODE ISLAND, 1940 (100 COPIES)

The Elements of Lettering is a limited edition of 100 copies and a very atypical design for the Press. The white wove paper, the rather large spine lettering, the marginal illustrations, and even the overall spacing, pagination, and binding suggest that Updike did not design this book. Despite the fact that it is a manual, which calls for a somewhat idiosyncratic arrangement, one has the feeling that the design was suggested by Benson himself.

In this publication, and several last volumes executed by him such as his *Some Aspects of Printing* and especially Van Wyck Brooks's *The Flowering of New England* done for the Limited Editions Club, Updike seems to be straining for a modern look. There is something formidable in the experiments of an octogenarian printer, but there is also something at variance with all other previous work created by Updike. He died weeks after Pearl Harbor, a little short of his eighty-second birthday. It was fortunate for him to have avoided a war he would have abhorred, and a new world which he and his sensibility might not have wished to experience.

SMITH 884

133. RECOLLECTIONS OF DANIEL BERKELEY UPDIKE, BY STANLEY MORISON AND RUDOLPH RUZICKA, WITH AN INTRODUCTION BY M. A. DE WOLFE HOWE
¶ BOSTON, CLUB OF ODD VOLUMES, 1943 (201 COPIES)

Perhaps the fact that the subject of this memorial volume not only concerned his late partner, whose absence in the midst of war Bianchi must have deeply felt, but also the fact that Morison, Ruzicka, and Howe were old and revered associates, inspired Bianchi to create a book that had the solidity and beauty which marked the best work of the Press. Printed in Janson on handmade paper, and bound in a specially executed Rosamond Loring paste-paper binding for the Club of Odd Volumes, this little volume is a touching and appropriate grace note to The Merrymount Press history. It was a note not sounded again.

SMITH 942

134. THE INAUGURAL ADDRESS OF FRANKLIN D. ROOSEVELT, PRESIDENT OF THE UNITED STATES
¶ WORCESTER, ACHILLE J. ST. ONGE, 1945 (2,000 COPIES)

The Merrymount Press printed very few miniature books, and all were executed for Achille St. Onge of Worcester, Massachusetts. This address is a serviceable, if unexceptional product, well-printed in Times Roman Monotype on Ecusta Bible paper.

SMITH 965

135. THE LOG OF CLEOPATRA'S BARGE II, 1928–1942
¶ BOSTON, PRIVATELY PRINTED, 1948

It is interesting to compare this book with *Cleopatra's Barge* (no. 53), executed thirty-five years earlier (also for Francis Crowninshield). The former logbook of the first yacht named "Cleopatra's Barge," on voyage between 1816–1817, attempts to capture some of the period flavor of the earlier nineteenth century. The latter volume, concerning as it does a contemporary "Cleopatra's Barge II" on voyage from 1925–1942, reproduces the log binding itself and evinces a modern spirit in design and typography. Yet the earlier volume has a marked charm and this latter seems a little overblown.

SMITH 1021

136. HANDBOOK OF THE MASSACHUSETTS HISTORICAL SOCIETY, 1791–1948
¶ BOSTON, MASSACHUSETTS, 1949

A few books designed by John Bianchi after the closing of The Merrymount Press in 1949 contain the Press's imprint. This *Handbook*, however, is the official last entry, number 1037, in the extended bibliography. (There are, in point of fact, numerous books that eluded both bibliographies.) This so-called last item is well-designed and printed, easy to read and to use. The *Handbook* coincidentally contains numerous references to the New England kin of D. B. Updike and even to the printer himself. All in all, an appropriate, symbolic, and dignified end.

SMITH 1037

The
GOVERNOR'S
Garden

A Relation of Some Paſſages in the Life of
His Excellency *Thomas Hutchinſon*, ſometime
Captain-General and Governor-in-Chief of
His Majeſty's Province of *Maſſachuſetts Bay.*

BY GEORGE R. R. RIVERS

Printed at *Boſton*, in *New England*, for
the Publiſhers, *Joſeph Knight Company*
in the Year of *Our Lord* MDCCCXCVI

BILL PRATT
THE SAW-BUCK PHILOSOPHER

AN APPRECIATION OF THE
LIFE, PUBLIC SERVICES, AND
SPEECHES OF ONE WHO FOR
OVER HALF A CENTURY
MINISTERED TO THE EN-
TERTAINMENT AND EDIFI-
CATION OF THE STUDENTS
OF WILLIAMS COLLEGE. BY
JOHN SHERIDAN ZELIE OF
THE CLASS OF 'EIGHTY-
SEVEN, AND CARROLL PERRY
OF THE CLASS OF 'NINETY.

WILLIAMSTOWN, MDCCCXCV.

about to cry again, when he was pre=

vented by the thought of the mess he

had made on the one=hundred=and=

sixty=seventh page. "And if I spoil

my own book, she will never look at

me, never." He sat down in despair.

❡ Chapter iii. ✠✠✠✠✠✠✠✠✠

Now it happened that at this moment

the young lady with whom he was in

love took up the book and began to

Merry- or four years before this time, there
mount came over one Captaine Wollas=
tone (a man of pretie parts), & with
him three or four more of some emi=
nencie, who brought with them a
great many servants, with provi=
sions & other implaments for to be=
ginne a plantation; and pitched them=
selves in a place within the Mas=
sachusets, which they called, after
their Captaine's name, Mount=
Wollaston. Amongst whom was
one Mr. Morton, who, it should
seem, had some small adventure (of
his owne or other mens) amongst
them." Morton, with the others,
settled at Wollaston, near Quin=
cy, calling his house Ma=re Mount,
or Merrymount; a name still at=
taching to that locality.

ABOUT the character of
Morton, opinions differ.
By some he is described as a roy=
stering, worthless fellow, who

made Merrymount the scene of con= Merry=
stant carousal and the home of the mount
idle ne'er=do=well. Others have
painted his picture as that of
an easy=going country gentleman,
more Cavalier than Roundhead in
his tendencies, whose attachment
to the Church of England led to
malignment by his Puritan neigh=
bours. Probably neither one nor yet
the other view is wholly true. But
it is true that he made Merrymount
the scene of old English sports,
and that he there set up a Maypole;
perhaps as a protest against the
gloomy fastings of the Puritans.
Morton, in that odd old book, The
New English Canaan, says that
"the Inhabitants of Pasonages=
sit, (having translated the name of
their habitation from that ancient
Salvage name to Ma=re Mount,
and being resolved to have the new
name confirmed for a memorial to
after ages,) did devise amongst

EASTER·DAY. THE COLLECT.

ALMIGHTY God, who through thine only-begotten Son Jesus Christ hast overcome death, and opened unto us the gate of everlasting life; We humbly beseech thee that, as by thy special grace preventing us thou dost put into our minds good desires, so by thy continual help we may bring the same to good effect; through Jesus Christ our Lord, who liveth and reigneth with thee and the Holy Ghost ever, one God, world without end. Amen.

THE EPISTLE. Col. iii. 1.

IF ye then be risen with Christ, seek those things which are above, where Christ sitteth on the right hand of God. Set your affection on things above, not on things on the earth. For ye are dead, and your life is hid with Christ in God. When Christ, who is our life, shall appear, then shall ye also appear with him in glory. Mortify therefore your members which are upon the earth; fornication, uncleanness, inordinate affection, evil concupiscence, and covetousness, which is idolatry: for which things' sake the wrath of God cometh on the children of disobedience: in the which ye also walked some time, when ye lived in them.

THE GOSPEL. St. John xx. 1.

THE first day of the week cometh Mary Magdalene early, when it was yet dark, unto the sepulchre, and seeth the stone taken away from the sepulchre. Then she runneth, and cometh to Simon Peter, and to the other disciple, whom Jesus loved, and saith unto them, They have taken away the Lord out of the sepulchre, and we know not where they have laid him. Peter therefore went forth, and that other disciple, and came to the sepulchre. So they ran both together: and the other disciple did outrun Peter, and came first to the sepulchre.

S·ATHANASIVS·DOCTOR
S·CHRYSOSTOMVS·DOCTOR
S·AVGVSTINVS·DOCTOR
S·HIERONYMVS·DOCTOR

S·MATTHAEVS·EVAN
S·MARCVS·EVANGE
S·LVCAS·EVANGEL
S·IOANNES·EVAI

BEATA·MARIA·VIRGO
S·MARIA·CLEOPHAE
S·MARIA·MAGDALENE

THE UNFOLDING LIFE

PASSAGES FROM THE DIARIES, NOTE-
BOOKS AND LETTERS OF HOWARD
MUNRO LONGYEAR, AND FROM THE
LETTERS HE RECEIVED FROM HIS
PARENTS AND FRIENDS. ARRANGED
AND EDITED BY HENRY D. NUNN

PRIVATELY PRINTED BY D. B. UPDIKE
THE MERRYMOUNT PRESS, BOSTON, IN
THE YEAR OF OUR LORD, MDCCCCI

lium, et lapis onychinus. Et nomen fluvii secundi Gehon;
ipse est qui circumit omnem terram Æthiopiæ. Nomen vero
fluminis tertii, Tygris; ipse vadit contra Assyrios. Fluvius
autem quartus, ipse est Euphrates. Tulit ergo Dominus
Deus hominem, et posuit eum in paradiso voluptatis, ut
operaretur, et custodiret illum. Præcepitque ei dicens: Ex
omni ligno paradisi comede: de ligno autem scientiæ boni
et mali ne comedas: in quocumque enim die comederis ex
eo, morte morieris. Dixit quoque Dominus Deus: Non est
bonum, esse hominem solum: faciamus ei adjutorium si-
mile sibi. Formatis igitur, Dominus Deus, de humo cunctis
animantibus terræ, et universis volatilibus cœli, adduxit ea
ad Adam, ut videret quid vocaret ea; omne enim quod vo-
cavit Adam animæ viventis, ipsum est nomen ejus. Appel-
lavitque Adam nominibus suis cuncta animantia, et uni-
versa volatilia cœli, et omnes bestias terræ; Adæ vero non
inveniebatur adjutor similis ejus. Immisit ergo Dominus
Deus soporem in Adam; cumque obdormisset, tulit unam
de costis ejus, et replevit carnem pro ea. Et ædificavit Dominus Deus costam, quam tulerat de Adam, in mulierem,
et adduxit eam ad Adam. Dixitque Adam: Hoc nunc os

ARCADY
IN
TROY

THE MERRYMOUNT PRESS BOSTON

THE POEMS OF
DANTE GABRIEL ROSSETTI
VOLUME I
THE BLESSED DAMOZEL
AND LONGER POEMS

THE PAFRAETS BOOK COMPANY
TROY NEW YORK

CORNELII TACITI DE VITA ET MORIBVS IVLII AGRICOLAE LIBER INCIPIT FELICITER

Larorum virorum facta moresque posteris tradere, antiquitus usita⟨
tum, ne nostris quidem temporibus quamquam incuriosa suorum
aetas omisit, quotiens magna aliqua ac nobilis virtus vicit ac super⟨
gressa est vitium parvis magnisque civitatibus commune, ignoran⟨
tiam recti et invidiam. sed apud priores, ut agere digna memoratu
pronum magisque in aperto erat, ita celeberrimus quisque ingenio
ad prodendam virtutis memoriam sine gratia aut ambitione bonae
tantum conscientiae pretio ducebatur. ac plerique suam ipsi vitam narrare fiduciam
potius morum quam adrogantiam arbitrati sunt, nec id Rutilio et Scauro citra fidem
aut obtrectationi fuit: adeo virtutes isdem temporibus optime aestimantur, quibus
facillime gignuntur. at nunc narraturo mihi vitam defuncti hominis venia opus fuit,
quam non petissem incusaturus tam saeva et infesta virtutibus tempora. Legimus,
cum Aruleno Rustico Paetus Thrasea, Herennio Senecioni Priscus Helvidius lau⟨
dati essent, capitale fuisse, neque in ipsos modo auctores, sed in libros quoque eorum
saevitum, delegato triumviris ministerio ut monumenta clarissimorum ingeniorum
in comitio ac foro urerentur. scilicet illo igne vocem populi Romani et libertatem
senatus et conscientiam generis humani aboleri arbitrabantur, expulsis insuper sa⟨
pientiae professoribus atque omni bona arte in exilium acta, ne quid usquam hone⟨
stum occurreret. dedimus profecto grande patientiae documentum; et sicut vetus
aetas vidit quid ultimum in libertate esset, ita nos quid in servitute, adempto per in⟨
quisitiones etiam loquendi audiendique commercio. memoriam quoque ipsam cum
voce perdidissemus, si tam in nostra potestate esset oblivisci quam tacere. Nunc de⟨
mum redit animus; et quamquam primo statim beatissimi saeculi ortu Nerva Cae⟨
sar res olim dissociabiles miscuerit, principatum ac libertatem, augeatque cotidie fe⟨
licitatem temporum Nerva Traianus, nec spem modo ac votum securitas publica,
sed ipsius voti fiduciam ac robur adsumpserit, natura tamen infirmitatis humanae
tardiora sunt remedia quam mala; et ut corpora nostra lente augescunt, cito extin⟨
guuntur, sic ingenia studiaque oppresseris facilius quam revocaveris: subit quippe
etiam ipsius inertiae dulcedo, et invisa primo desidia postremo amatur. quid? si per
quindecim annos, grande mortalis aevi spatium, multi fortuitis casibus, promptissi⟨
mus quisque saevitia principis interciderunt, pauci, et, ut ita dixerim, non modo alio⟨
rum sed etiam nostri superstites sumus, exemptis e media vita tot annis, quibus iu⟨
venes ad senectutem, senes prope ad ipsos exactae aetatis terminos per silentium ve⟨
nimus. non tamen pigebit vel incondita ac rudi voce memoriam prioris servitutis ac
testimonium praesentium bonorum composuisse. hic interim liber, honori Agricolae
soceri mei destinatus, professione pietatis aut laudatus erit aut excusatus.
Gnaeus Iulius Agricola, vetere et inlustri Foroiuliensium colonia ortus, utrumque
avum procuratorem Caesarum habuit, quae equestris nobilitas est. pater illi Iulius
Graecinus, senatorii ordinis, studio eloquentiae sapientiaeque notus, iisque ipsis vir⟨
tutibus iram Gai Caesaris meritus: namque M. Silanum accusare iussus et, quia ab⟨
nuerat, interfectus est. mater Iulia Procilla fuit, rarae castitatis. in huius sinu indul⟨
gentiaque educatus per omnem honestarum artium cultum pueritiam adulescen⟨
tiamque transegit. arcebat eum ab inlecebris peccantium praeter ipsius bonam inte⟨
gramque naturam, quod statim parvulus sedem ac magistram studiorum Massiliam
habuit, locum Graeca comitate et provinciali parsimonia mixtum ac bene composi⟨
tum. memoria teneo solitum ipsum narrare se prima in iuventa studium philosophiae

37. CELLINI 1906

11. HOLY ISLAND CATHEDRAL
DRAWN AND ETCHED BY J. M. W. TURNER
ENGRAVED BY CHARLES TURNER

THE ETCHING

In lower margin, scratched in open Roman letters: "Holy-Island [*space*] Northd." Signed by Charles Turner. *Sepia.*

From the Rawlinson Collection.

ENGRAVER'S PROOFS

1. Title as before. *Sepia.*

From the Stokes Collection.

2. Lettered as in first published state. Signed by Charles Turner. *Golden brown ink.*

From the Hawkins and Rawlinson Collections.

PUBLISHED STATE

FIRST STATE

Many high lights added on masonry and in foreground. Initial letter (A) and letters of title open capitals. *Sepia.*

[25]

HISTORIE OF THE LIFE AND DEATH OF
Sir William Kirkaldy
❦ of Grange, Knight ❧

WHEREIN *is declared his many Wise Designs and Valiant Actions, with a True Relation of his Heroic Conduct in the Castle of Edinburgh which he had the Honour to defend for the Queen of Scots. Now set forth from Authentic Sources by* HAROLD MURDOCK.

PRINTED *for* The Club of Odd Volumes *at* BOSTON *in* NEW ENGLAND *in the Year of Our Lord,* MDCCCCVI

Intel-
lect
vine aspects until it finds satisfaction; and since the intellect is one of the tones of our soul, by means of the soul it composes the form of the body where it dwells, according to its volition. And when it has to reproduce a human body, it takes pleasure in repeating the body which it originally created; whence it follows that they who fall in love are prone to become enamoured of what resembles them.

74.

Of the
Senses
There are the four powers: memory, intellect, sensuality and lust. The first two are intellectual, the others sensual. Of the five senses, sight, hearing, smell are with difficulty prevented; touch and taste not at all. Taste follows smell in the case of dogs and other greedy animals.

75.

Why does the eye perceive things more clearly in dreams than with the imagination when one is awake?

76.

Time
Although time is included among continuous quantities, being indivisible and immaterial it does not altogether fall into the scope of geo-metry, — by which it is divided into figures and bodies of infinite variety, which are seen to be continuous inasmuch as they are visible and ma-terial, — but it agrees only with its first principles,

30

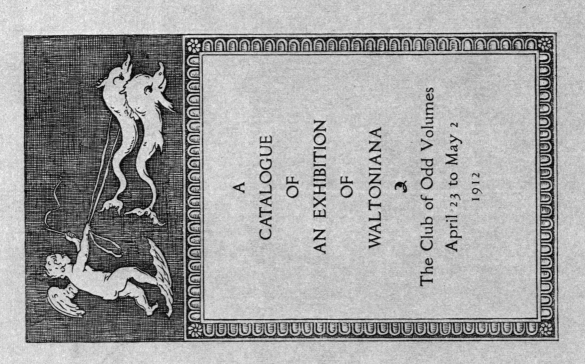

A
CATALOGUE
OF
AN EXHIBITION
OF
WALTONIANA

The Club of Odd Volumes
April 23 to May 2
1912

LETTERS
OF
BULWER-LYTTON TO MACREADY

With an Introduction by
Brander Matthews

1836–1866

PRIVATELY PRINTED
THE CARTERET BOOK CLUB
NEWARK, NEW JERSEY
1911

NEWARK

A SERIES OF ENGRAVINGS ON WOOD BY

RUDOLPH RUZICKA

WITH AN APPRECIATION OF

THE PICTORIAL ASPECTS OF THE TOWN

BY WALTER PRICHARD EATON

THE CARTERET BOOK CLUB

NEWARK · NEW JERSEY

1917

Portraits of Whistler

A CRITICAL STUDY AND AN ICONOGRAPHY

BY A. E. GALLATIN

WITH FORTY ILLUSTRATIONS

*Often I have found a portrait superior in real
instruction to half a dozen biographies.* CARLYLE

NEW YORK: JOHN LANE COMPANY

LONDON: JOHN LANE, THE BODLEY HEAD

1918

Bibliotheca Americana

CATALOGUE OF THE

John Carter Brown Library

IN BROWN UNIVERSITY

Providence, Rhode Island

VOLUME I

PROVIDENCE

Published by the Library

1919

A CHOICE OF MANUSCRIPTS
AND BOOKBINDINGS
FROM
THE LIBRARY OF
ISABELLA STEWART GARDNER
FENWAY COURT

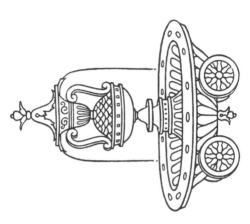

MDCCCCXXII

The Felicities of
Sixty

By ISAAC H. LIONBERGER

BOSTON
The Club of Odd Volumes
1922

BENJAMIN FRANKLIN
ON BALLOONS

A LETTER WRITTEN FROM PASSY, FRANCE, JANUARY SIXTEENTH

MDCCLXXXIV

"Convincing Sovereigns of the Folly of Wars, may perhaps be one Effect of it"

VUE DE LA TERRASSE DE M. FRANKLIN A PASSY.

PRIVATELY PRINTED FOR HIS FRIENDS BY W. K. BIXBY

SAINT LOUIS: MDCCCCXXII

75. THE JOURNAL OF MRS. JOHN AMORY 1923

DEDICATION OF THE
WEST WINDOW OF ST. JOHN'S CHURCH
BEVERLY FARMS

᭒᭙᭒

THE West Window of St. John's Church, Beverly Farms, in memory of Mrs. William Caleb Loring, was dedicated at the morning service on Whitsunday, 1925.

The Processional Hymn was:

I HEARD a sound of voices
　　Around the great white throne,
With harpers harping on their harps
　　To Him that sat thereon:
"Salvation, glory, honour!"
　　I heard the song arise,
As through the courts of heaven it rolled
　　In wondrous harmonies.

From every clime and kindred,
　　And nations from afar,
As serried ranks returning home
　　In triumph from a war,
I heard the saints upraising,
　　The myriad hosts among,
In praise of Him who died and lives,
　　Their one glad triumph song.

I

THE FORM OF
CONSECRATION OF
ST. GEORGE'S CHAPEL
APRIL XXIII, ANNO DOMINI
MDCCCCXXVII

ST. GEORGE'S SCHOOL
MIDDLETOWN, RHODE ISLAND

93 · THE FORM OF CONSECRATION OF ST. GEORGE'S CHAPEL 1928

STEPHEN CRANE
BY
Thomas L. Raymond

NEWARK NEW JERSEY
The Carteret Book Club
1923

76. STEPHEN CRANE 1923

WAR BOOKS

By
H. M. TOMLINSON

A Lecture
Given at Manchester University
February 15, 1929

THE ROWFANT CLUB
Cleveland, Ohio
1930

QUARTO CLUB PAPERS

MCMXXVII–MCMXXVIII

NEW YORK

PRINTED FOR THE MEMBERS

MCMXXIX

Morning Prayer

¶ Or this Psalm.

Jubilate Deo. Psalm c.

O BE joyful in the LORD, all ye lands: * serve the LORD with gladness, and come before his presence with a song.

Be ye sure that the LORD he is God; it is he that hath made us, and not we ourselves; * we are his people, and the sheep of his pasture.

O go your way into his gates with thanksgiving, and into his courts with praise; * be thankful unto him, and speak good of his Name.

For the LORD is gracious, his mercy is everlasting; * and his truth endureth from generation to generation.

¶ Then shall be said the Apostles' Creed by the Minister and the People, standing. And any Churches may, instead of the words, He descended into hell, use the words, He went into the place of departed spirits, which are considered as words of the same meaning in the Creed.

I BELIEVE in God the Father Almighty, Maker of heaven and earth:

And in Jesus Christ his only Son our Lord: Who was conceived by the Holy Ghost, Born of the Virgin Mary: Suffered under Pontius Pilate, Was crucified, dead, and buried: He descended into hell; The third day he rose again from the dead: He ascended into heaven, And sitteth on the right hand of God the Father Almighty: From thence he shall come to judge the quick and the dead.

I believe in the Holy Ghost: The holy Catholic Church; The Communion of Saints: The Forgiveness of sins: The Resurrection of the body: And the Life everlasting. Amen.

¶ Or the Creed commonly called the Nicene.

I BELIEVE in one God the Father Almighty, Maker of heaven and earth, And of all things visible and invisible:

15

THE BOOK OF
COMMON PRAYER

and Administration of the Sacraments
and Other Rites and Ceremonies
of the Church

ACCORDING TO THE USE OF THE
PROTESTANT EPISCOPAL CHURCH
IN THE UNITED STATES OF AMERICA

Together with The Psalter
or Psalms of David

PRINTED FOR THE COMMISSION

A. D. MDCCCCXXVIII

POEMS TO VERA

BY

GEORGE STERLING

NEW YORK

OXFORD UNIVERSITY PRESS

1938

126. POEMS TO VERA 1938

The Life of
Our Lord

Written during the Years 1846–1849

By Charles Dickens
for His Children
And now first published

New York
Simon and Schuster
1934

114. THE LIFE OF OUR LORD 1934

THE
PREFACE
TO
Johnson's
DICTIONARY
OF THE
English Language
1755

CLEVELAND

THE ROWFANT CLUB

1934

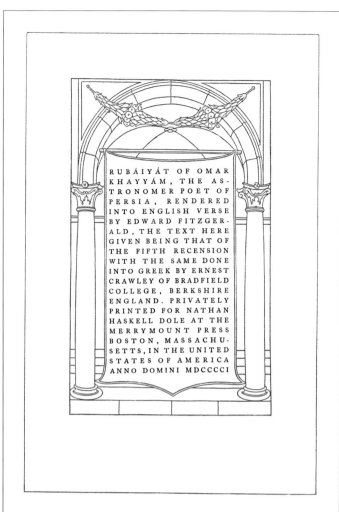

RUBÁIYÁT OF OMAR
KHAYYÁM, THE AS-
TRONOMER POET OF
PERSIA, RENDERED
INTO ENGLISH VERSE
BY EDWARD FITZGER-
ALD, THE TEXT HERE
GIVEN BEING THAT OF
THE FIFTH RECENSION
WITH THE SAME DONE
INTO GREEK BY ERNEST
CRAWLEY OF BRADFIELD
COLLEGE, BERKSHIRE
ENGLAND. PRIVATELY
PRINTED FOR NATHAN
HASKELL DOLE AT THE
MERRYMOUNT PRESS
BOSTON, MASSACHU-
SETTS, IN THE UNITED
STATES OF AMERICA
ANNO DOMINI MDCCCCI

HOWES

My customers say, when I cleanse a garment, that somehow I bring the bloom back to it

HOWES

[*over*

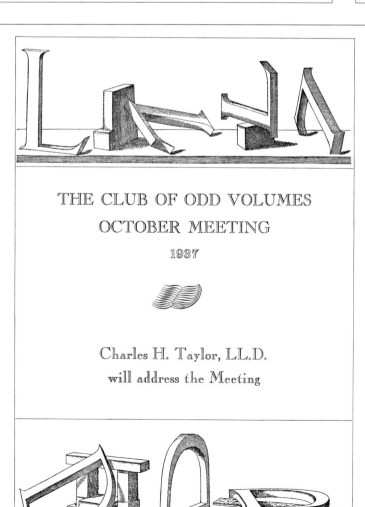

THE CLUB OF ODD VOLUMES

OCTOBER MEETING

1937

Charles H. Taylor, LL.D.

will address the Meeting

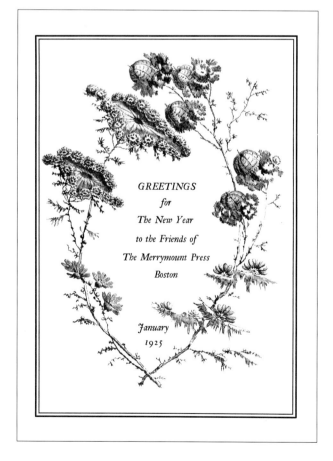

GREETINGS
for
The New Year
to the Friends of
The Merrymount Press
Boston

January
1925

VARIOUS EPHEMERA

Carried as follows: Sheets, Envelopes and Single and Short-fold Cards in Café Royale, Celeste Blue, Napier Gray, Cockade White, Rose Marie

When ordering, please give name and size as listed above. Also state color, and specify whether Sheets, Cards or Envelopes. Colors listed in order shown.

LINWEAVE
◈ FRENCH DECKLE
◈ SIZE: BEAUCAIRE

Signora Maria Pamphili
ANNOUNCES A CONCERT TO BE HELD AT
LA GRANJA, PALM BEACH
MARCH 20, 1925, AT NINE P.M.

Programme

Die Junge Nonne	*Schubert*
Alinde	*Schubert*
O Nachtigall	*Brahms*
Louise	*H. Gray*
Adieu pour jamais	*Loeffler*
Maja dolorosa	*Granados*
Old Italian Folk-Songs:	
Harvest Song	*Sicilian*
Carnival Song	*Neapolitan*
Lullaby	*Umbrian*

Tickets $5.00 each

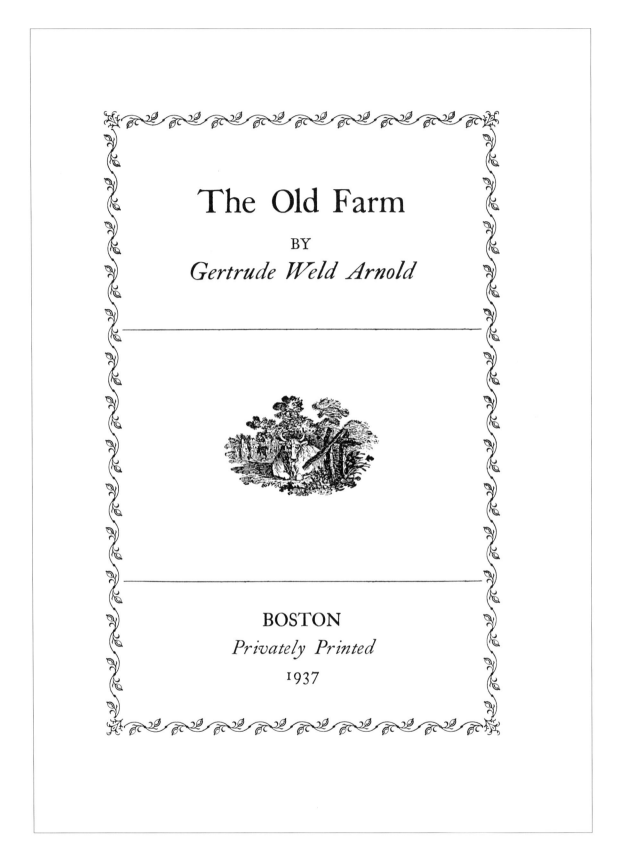

The Old Farm

BY

Gertrude Weld Arnold

BOSTON

Privately Printed

1937

LIST OF ILLUSTRATIONS

. .

With the exception of the illustrations marked below with an asterisk, all reproductions are actual size. The page formats indicated by a rule do not necessarily reflect the original page size and margins.

CHRONOLOGY
· ·

1860   Daniel Berkeley Updike born to Caesar Augustus and Elizabeth Bigelow Adams Updike in Providence, Rhode Island, on February 24

1874   John Bianchi born in Renasso, Italy

1877   Caesar Augustus Updike dies

1878   Updike becomes temporary assistant to the librarian of the Providence Athenaeum

1880   At the instance of a relative, Updike commences work at Houghton Mifflin, Boston, as an errand boy

1890   Transferred to The Riverside Press in Cambridge

1891   Writes and publishes with Harold Brown *On the Dedication of American Churches*

1892   Commission to arrange the decorations and borders for *The Book of Common Prayer* of 1892, printed by T. L. De Vinne

1893   Leaves The Riverside Press and opens independent offices at 6 Beacon Street as "Typographic advisor"

        Vexilla Regis Quotidie, first book issued

        Becomes member of The Grolier Club

        Begins work on *The Altar Book*

        John Bianchi joins firm

1895   Elizabeth Updike dies

1896   Moves office around the corner to Tremont Place

        The first work of 1896, a pamphlet, *In Memory of Martin Brimmer*, bears the name "The Merrymount Press" for the first time

        Acquires first type, Caslon, with which *The Governor's Garden* becomes the first book actually set at the Press

        The Altar Book is published

        Meets Bruce Rogers

1898   Press moves to 104 Chestnut Street where a single press is installed

1903   Press moves to 232 Summer Street where it acquires major printing presses

        T. M. Cleland does first work for the Press

1906   "The Humanists' Library," first series, inaugurated

1907   W. A. Dwiggins and Rudolph Ruzicka do first work for the Press

1911   Updike begins a series of lectures on printing at Harvard

1912   Ruzicka executes first of his Merrymount Press New Year's cards

1915   John Bianchi taken into partnership

1922   Publication of *Printing Types*

1924   Updike meets Stanley Morison

1926   Updike becomes an honorary member of The Grolier Club

1928   35th Anniversary exhibition of 77 Merrymount Press imprints at A.I.G.A. in New York

       Competition entered by the Press for the printing of *The Book of Common Prayer* of 1928, and subsequently won

1929   Harvard University confers an honorary Master of Arts degree on Updike

1930   *The Book of Common Prayer* issued

1931   Exhibition of Merrymount Press work at Goodspeed's Book Shop, Boston. Exhibition of 43 Merrymount Press works from the Collection of Max Farrand at the Zamorano Club, San Marino

1935   Exhibition of over 200 volumes of The Merrymount Press in the Treasure Room of the Boston Public Library

1940   Major exhibition of some 500 Merrymount Press imprints sponsored by A.I.G.A and The Grolier Club, held at the Club in New York

       Exhibition of Merrymount Press imprints at the Boston Public Library

1941   Updike dies December 29

1942   Updike Memorial exhibition of 68 Merrymount Press books at the Huntington Library, San Marino

       Memorial exhibition also at the Club of Odd Volumes, Boston

1943   Exhibition of 63 Merrymount Press books at the Roxburghe Club, San Francisco

1949   The Merrymount Press ceases operation

TYPES USED AT THE MERRYMOUNT PRESS

· ·

As will be seen, the number of types used by the Press shows little variety. For most books, Caslon, Scotch-face, in the Mountjoye-Oxford combinations of founts is the best, and a departure is desirable only when a new type performs the task to be done better than these types can. But new material—borders, initial letters, and type ornaments with which to vary the effect of the types used—was all along acquired, some of it during my several journeys abroad. . . . 'The new should be welcome, the old not forgotten.'

Daniel Berkeley Updike
NOTES

YEAR INTRODUCED	TYPE	FREQUENCY	
1894	Caslon	275	} 467
1926	Monotype Caslon	192	
1897	Scotch-Face	171	} 190
1935	Monotype Scotch-Face	19	
1910	Oxford	122	
1903	Mountjoye	72	
1918	Janson	63	
1939	Monotype Times Roman	61	
1936	Monotype Baskerville	32	
1896	Clarendon	31	
1903	Montallegro	12	
1893	Modernized Old Style	11	
1939	Monotype Bulmer	11	
1924	Poliphilus	8	
1927	Lutetia	8	
1939	Perpetua Titling	8	
1898	Black-Letter	6	
1896	Merrymount	5	
1925	Blado	4	
1901	Batarde	3	
1898	XVII Century Old Style	2	
1900	Caslon Black-Letter	2	
1930	Bodoni	2	
1933	Granjon	2	
1899	Modern-Face, Italic	1	
1901	Caslon Italic	1	
1922	Old Style	1	
1933	Garamond	1	
1934	Lettre Batarde	1	
1938	Monotype Cheltenham	1	
1939	Bembo	1	
1940	Astrée	1	
1942	Tudor Black	1	

[75]

COMMERCIAL PUBLISHING HOUSES ASSOCIATED
WITH THE MERRYMOUNT PRESS
· ·

The list below includes only commercial publishing houses for whom publishing constituted their major business. Bookstores, book clubs, libraries, foundations, part-time publishers, private presses, or even The Merrymount Press and Updike are not included. The publishers are listed in chronological order of commission.

RAPHAEL TUCK AND COMPANY, LTD., NEW YORK

JAMES POTT AND COMPANY, NEW YORK

JOSEPH KNIGHT AND COMPANY, BOSTON

THOMAS Y. CROWELL AND COMPANY, NEW YORK AND BOSTON

LONGMANS, GREEN AND COMPANY, LONDON AND BOMBAY

R. H. RUSSELL, NEW YORK

DODD, MEAD AND COMPANY, NEW YORK

CHARLES SCRIBNER'S SONS, NEW YORK

D. APPLETON AND COMPANY, NEW YORK

L. C. PAGE AND COMPANY, INC., BOSTON

G. SCHIRMER, NEW YORK

D. C. HEATH AND COMPANY, BOSTON

DOUBLEDAY, PAGE AND COMPANY, NEW YORK

McCLURE, PHILLIPS AND COMPANY, NEW YORK

A. C. McCLURG AND COMPANY, CHICAGO

JOHN LANE, LONDON AND NEW YORK

THE MACMILLAN COMPANY, LONDON AND NEW YORK

THE CENTURY COMPANY, NEW YORK

GINN AND COMPANY, BOSTON

E. P. DUTTON AND COMPANY, NEW YORK

OLIVER DITSON COMPANY, BOSTON

ELKIN MATTHEWS, LONDON

THE CENTURY COMPANY, NEW YORK

R. H. HINKLEY COMPANY, BOSTON

JOHN W. LUCE AND COMPANY, BOSTON AND LONDON

WORLD BOOK COMPANY, YONKERS

MOFFAT, YARD AND COMPANY, NEW YORK

CHARLES H. DITSON AND COMPANY, NEW YORK AND PHILADELPHIA

W. B. CLARKE COMPANY, BOSTON

OXFORD UNIVERSITY PRESS (HUMPHREY MILFORD), LONDON

YALE UNIVERSITY PRESS, NEW HAVEN

BELL AND COCKBURN, TORONTO

COLUMBIA UNIVERSITY PRESS, NEW YORK

THE ATLANTIC MONTHLY PRESS, BOSTON

HARVARD UNIVERSITY PRESS, CAMBRIDGE

DUFFIELD AND COMPANY, NEW YORK

HARCOURT, BRACE AND COMPANY, NEW YORK
THE JOHN DAY COMPANY, NEW YORK
ALFRED A. KNOPF, NEW YORK
HENRY HOLT AND COMPANY, NEW YORK
R. R. BOWKER COMPANY, NEW YORK
DOUBLEDAY, DORAN AND COMPANY, GARDEN CITY
RIMINGTON AND HOOPER, NEW YORK
RANDOM HOUSE, NEW YORK
CONSTABLE AND COMPANY, NEW YORK
G. & C. MERRIAM COMPANY, SPRINGFIELD
SIMON AND SCHUSTER, NEW YORK
WILLIAM HEINEMANN LTD., LONDON
THE CHRISTIAN SCIENCE PUBLISHING SOCIETY, BOSTON
FUNK AND WAGNALLS COMPANY, NEW YORK AND LONDON
LITTLE, BROWN AND COMPANY, BOSTON
NOBLE AND NOBLE PUBLISHERS, INC., NEW YORK
MOREHOUSE-GORHAM COMPANY, NEW YORK

¶ 1,500 COPIES OF THIS CATALOGUE HAVE BEEN PRINTED
IN ADOBE CASLON TYPE ON MONADNOCK CARESS PAPER
AT THE STINEHOUR PRESS, IN LUNENBURG, VERMONT.
DESIGNED BY JERRY KELLY.